365 Days of the Buddha's Wisdom

365 Days of the Buddha's Wisdom

A Personal Journal of Your Journey

Cristo López, Ph.D.

*Dedicated to Bubu, who exemplifies loving-kindness at all times,
and to Ary, whose compassion and kindness know no bounds.*

PREFACE

Almost forty years ago, I found myself amid a spiritual crisis. I had been raised a Roman Catholic, attended Catholic school, and assumed that all the teaching that the Church presented to me was inerrant and trustworthy.

As I grew a bit older, I began to have doubts. I found inconsistencies in the bible that bothered me. When I sought clarification from my teachers and clergy, more often than not, my questions were rebuffed instead of taken seriously. On more than one occasion, they told me that the very act of raising questions was, in fact, *harmful* to me and my faith; I should just accept the teachings and banish all doubt and questions from my mind.

This approach to my spiritual life didn't sit well with me and led me to conclude that something was seriously amiss. If I couldn't question the facts and tenets around my faith, was I anything more than a blind follower? That's not something that I could accept about myself, especially since one of the most important things I learned from my parents was the notion of self-responsibility and self-actualization.

Now I hope that you will understand something important. I am not an enemy of any particular organized religion. But I believe that each of us has to find our path to the truth and meaning of our existence with all my heart. It is not for me to judge anyone else's path. If their efforts are sincere, and if their faith brings them joy and happiness and brings no harm to others, I have no interest in changing their path.

My path ultimately led me to the teachings of the Buddha. I was attracted to Buddhism because it emphasized the necessity of self-responsibility in all things. More than that, I was drawn to the promise that joy and happiness were already an innate part of each one of us. With practice and devotion to loving-kindness and compassion, we could experience joy and happiness, even amidst times of turmoil or sadness. This path just felt right to me.

I went on to study philosophy (among other things) and earned BA., MA., and Ph.D. degrees. I consider myself a "secular" Buddhist, meaning that I am drawn to the deep wisdom found in the Buddha's teachings, but avoid any supernatural beliefs that harken back to traditional formal religions.

I was inspired to create this book by my first teacher, a Korean Buddhist monk, who taught me that our search for peace, love, and happiness required daily practice. Along with meditation, he encouraged me to read from the Buddha's teachings every morning and pick one piece of wisdom to contemplate throughout the day. He also encouraged me to reflect by writing down my thoughts in a journal actively.

I did as he instructed and found that spending just a few minutes reflecting and writing helped me live more in the moment and kept me attuned to the opportunities to be compassionate and loving throughout the day. Eventually, I simplified my journal and created the writing template you'll find within.

The format is simple but effective. At the top, you will find a quote from the Buddha, followed by a brief sentence or paragraph of my commentary. My comments are not to be considered definitive; I wrote them solely to trigger the reader's imagination and perhaps provide a launching pad for their self-discovery.

What follows are three prompts:

1. "This quote inspires the following thoughts in me:"
2. "This quote inspires me to take these actions today:"
3. "Before bedtime) I accomplished these actions today:"

Although there are 365 quotes to be contemplated, I did not intend for the journal writer to proceed chronologically from page one to the end (unless they want to). I suggest that the reader randomly flip through the book and stop whenever a quote strikes them at the moment. Spontaneity often leads to unexpected but timely insights and feels more fun and playful. But please proceed as you feel most comfortable!

Finally, I'd like to thank you for purchasing this book. My sincere wish is that it helps you reach the happiness you deserve and exude compassion for all others in your life.

Mostly, I hope it helps you realize your potential to become a Buddha in your own right.

Peace.

Cristo López

"If anything is worth doing, do it with all your heart."
- The Buddha

For some people, things are worth doing only if they are done with all their heart. They choose to make themselves vulnerable in order to experience the reward that comes with completing something worthwhile. Others feel that it's better to keep safe and go through life without any major risks. Although this may be comforting, it can cause one to miss out on life's most fulfilling moments.

Today's Date:

This quote inspires the following thoughts in me:

This quote inspires me to take these actions today:

(Before bedtime) I accomplished these actions today:

"If we fail to look after others when they need help, who will look after us?" - The Buddha

As the world becomes more divided and people become more disconnected, it is up to us to look out for our fellow man. We all know someone who is struggling in some way, whether it is through addiction, joblessness, poverty or mental health issues. It is crucial that we don't turn a blind eye to the struggles of others; if we do, then no one will be looking out for us when we need help.

Today's Date:

This quote inspires the following thoughts in me:

This quote inspires me to take these actions today:

(Before bedtime) I accomplished these actions today:

"To live a pure unselfish life, one must count nothing as one's own in the midst of abundance." - The Buddha

Many of us have heard the saying, "Count your blessings." But what does that really mean? What are we supposed to count? Is it just easily documented, tangible things or is it just anything that's in our hearts that brings contentment and joy?

Today's Date:

<u>This quote inspires the following thoughts in me:</u>

<u>This quote inspires me to take these actions today:</u>

<u>(Before bedtime) I accomplished these actions today:</u>

"Nothing ever exists entirely alone; everything is in relation to everything else." - The Buddha

The idea that nothing exists alone is a concept that can be both liberating and distressing, depending on the context. In some cases, this realization can lead to greater compassion for others who share our problems. On the other hand, it may also be difficult to see past our own problems when everything seems so interconnected.

Today's Date:

This quote inspires the following thoughts in me:

This quote inspires me to take these actions today:

(Before bedtime) I accomplished these actions today:

"Love is a gift of one's inner most soul to another so both can be whole." - The Buddha

The act of loving someone is the act of letting them see who you are, not who they want you to be. It's an act of vulnerability and honesty. Loving someone means putting their needs over your own so they can feel loved and secure in themselves. It means accepting their past mistakes with understanding and patience, because you know they will do anything for you.

Today's Date:

This quote inspires the following thoughts in me:

This quote inspires me to take these actions today:

(Before bedtime) I accomplished these actions today:

"There is no path to happiness: happiness is the path."
- The Buddha

Happiness is not a destination that you can reach, but instead it is the journey that you take. Happiness is something that we don't achieve and then stop striving for, because the very act of striving for happiness makes us happy. Humans are social animals and we need to live in community, to be happy; this is why we need to love and care for each other. Happiness comes from within - we can't rely on other people or our possessions to make us happy.

Today's Date:

This quote inspires the following thoughts in me:

This quote inspires me to take these actions today:

(Before bedtime) I accomplished these actions today:

"Set your heart on doing good. Do it over and over again, and you will be filled with joy." - The Buddha

There's no better way to be happy than to do good things for others. When we do something kind, we should always think about how it will make the other person feel and not only how it will make us feel. Doing good makes people happy and fills them with joy. What good do you plan to do today?

Today's Date:

This quote inspires the following thoughts in me:

This quote inspires me to take these actions today:

(Before bedtime) I accomplished these actions today:

"Those who are free of resentful thoughts surely find peace." - The Buddha

Freedom from thoughts of resentment is a feat that many strive for. Those who are free from thoughts of anger and resentment find peace in their environments, as well as within themselves. In order to attain this goal, one must first recognize the difference between sadness and anger. Sadness comes from a place of being hurt or disappointed by other people, whereas anger arises out of frustration with oneself.

Today's Date:

This quote inspires the following thoughts in me:

This quote inspires me to take these actions today:

(Before bedtime) I accomplished these actions today:

"Work out your own salvation. Do not depend on others." - The Buddha

We all want what is best for ourselves, and yet we find ourselves depending on others to get the things we want. But what would happen if we took responsibility for our own lives? If we changed our behavior and habits and did the work necessary to get into a better place in life, then we could work towards achieving all of our dreams.

Today's Date:

This quote inspires the following thoughts in me:

This quote inspires me to take these actions today:

(Before bedtime) I accomplished these actions today:

"If you knew what I know about the power of giving, you would not let a single meal pass without sharing it in some way." - The Buddha

When you think about the power of giving, do you think about what you can get in return? What's in it for me? How will I benefit from it? Or, do you think about the impact your actions will make on other people?

Today's Date:

This quote inspires the following thoughts in me:

This quote inspires me to take these actions today:

(Before bedtime) I accomplished these actions today:

"Better than a thousand hollow words, is one word that brings peace." - The Buddha

The words that matter the most are not the words that merely sound nice. The words that come directly from your heart and can change someone's perspective in an instant are the ones that carry the most value.

Today's Date:

This quote inspires the following thoughts in me:

This quote inspires me to take these actions today:

(Before bedtime) I accomplished these actions today:

"We are what we think. All that we are arises with our thoughts. With our thoughts, we make the world."
- The Buddha

Buddhism teaches that the world is an illusion, yet it may be possible that everything in our lives are illusions because of our thoughts. It's said that all things come from the mind, but more importantly, it's what we think that separates us from others. The teachings also say that the mind is reality and the only reality. If this is true, then what happens when we think differently?

Today's Date:

This quote inspires the following thoughts in me:

This quote inspires me to take these actions today:

(Before bedtime) I accomplished these actions today:

"The tongue is like a sharp knife. It may kill without drawing blood." - The Buddha

A cutting word that penetrates into a person's soul and never leaves will do the job just as well. The words may have been spoken years ago, but they still linger, bruising the person's heart and soul with each breath, destroying any hope of peace or happiness. Shouldn't we think carefully before we speak, so as to avoid doing any such harm?

Today's Date:

This quote inspires the following thoughts in me:

This quote inspires me to take these actions today:

(Before bedtime) I accomplished these actions today:

"One moment can change a day, one day can change a life and one life can change the world." - The Buddha

Each of us has that one moment that will shape who we are and who we will become. We may not be able to control the cosmos but we do have the power and ability to control our lives and make each moment count. The second most important decision we make is what we do with our time, so let's use it wisely and never give up on ourselves or others.

Today's Date:

This quote inspires the following thoughts in me:

This quote inspires me to take these actions today:

(Before bedtime) I accomplished these actions today:

"Kindness should become the natural way of life, not the exception." - The Buddha

When someone does a good deed for others, they make the world a better place. This makes people want to do more good deeds, and it can create a chain reaction of goodness as those who were helped may make an effort to help others as well. It is rare these days to see someone doing something nice for strangers, however, everyone should be striving for this kind of life.

Today's Date:

This quote inspires the following thoughts in me:

This quote inspires me to take these actions today:

(Before bedtime) I accomplished these actions today:

"It is a man's own mind, not his enemy or foe, that lures him to evil ways." - The Buddha

We are our own adversaries. Yes, there are forces outside of us that try to lure us down the wrong path, but it is ultimately our own mind that convinces us to do evil. We are enticed by desires, deceived by appearances, overpowered by impulses. Our will succumbs to temptation and evil conquers good. How do you guard against this?

Today's Date:

This quote inspires the following thoughts in me:

This quote inspires me to take these actions today:

(Before bedtime) I accomplished these actions today:

"Happiness comes when your work and words are of benefit to yourself and others." - The Buddha

Everyone is looking to be happy. However, true happiness doesn't come from the outside, but rather it comes from within. Happiness can be attained by finding what lies in your heart. Do that, and share it. You'll find happiness in whatever you do with your day.

Today's Date:

This quote inspires the following thoughts in me:

This quote inspires me to take these actions today:

(Before bedtime) I accomplished these actions today:

"An idea that is developed and put into action is more important than an idea that exists only as an idea."
- The Buddha

We all know that ideas are only worth the paper they're written on until they come to life. Ideas are just thoughts in someone's head that need to be developed before anyone can really understand how good it is. What is the point of a great idea if it never becomes something?

Today's Date:

This quote inspires the following thoughts in me:

This quote inspires me to take these actions today:

(Before bedtime) I accomplished these actions today:

"Just as a mother would protect her only child with her life, even so let one cultivate a boundless love towards all beings." - The Buddha

Have you ever had someone who loved you more than anything in the world? Have you ever felt that they would do anything to protect you? That is how one should feel towards all beings. If everyone trained themselves to have this perspective then peace and happiness would surely dominate the world.

Today's Date:

This quote inspires the following thoughts in me:

This quote inspires me to take these actions today:

(Before bedtime) I accomplished these actions today:

"Just as a candle cannot burn without fire, men cannot live without a spiritual life." - The Buddha

In order for us to live a fulfilling life, we must find meaning and purpose. We cannot ignore our spiritual side and never try to find answers for our existence. It is important to go on this journey of self-exploration so that we may be able to find meaning and purpose.

Today's Date:

This quote inspires the following thoughts in me:

This quote inspires me to take these actions today:

(Before bedtime) I accomplished these actions today:

"Resolutely train yourself to attain peace."
- The Buddha

As the old saying goes, 'You get what you give.' The reason for this is that our own actions will always reflect back on us. The proverb suggests that if we want to be happy, we need to focus on nurturing positive qualities of ourselves and be thoughtful of how our actions influence others. What steps can you take today to get started?

Today's Date:

This quote inspires the following thoughts in me:

This quote inspires me to take these actions today:

(Before bedtime) I accomplished these actions today:

"There is no fear for one whose mind is not filled with desires." - The Buddha

There is no fear for one whose mind is not filled with desires, for death can't touch him. One who desires for nothing has nothing to lose, so there are many things that are within his power. He's more likely to be able to rise to any difficulty he faces, because he knows that there are ways out of it.

Today's Date:

This quote inspires the following thoughts in me:

This quote inspires me to take these actions today:

(Before bedtime) I accomplished these actions today:

"Wear your ego like a loose fitting garment."
- The Buddha

We often don't notice the power of our own self-centered feelings and thoughts, but we're constantly projecting them onto those around us. If we want to be effective leaders and members of communities, we must first learn to manage these thoughts and feelings. It's not just about humility - it's about awareness that other people have their own needs and pain, and that can't always be helped by the way you spun the situation in your head.

Today's Date:

This quote inspires the following thoughts in me:

This quote inspires me to take these actions today:

(Before bedtime) I accomplished these actions today:

"Even death is not to be feared by one who has lived wisely." - The Buddha

Death is something that none of us can escape. Yet, for those who have lived wisely, the prospect of death has no sting to it. They are free from the pain and the fear that grips most people when faced with their eventual end. The wise person understands that death does not change anything about them; they will always be the same person they were before they died. It is this understanding, coupled with a life lived well, which allows them to face death with an air of calm acceptance.

Today's Date:

This quote inspires the following thoughts in me:

This quote inspires me to take these actions today:

(Before bedtime) I accomplished these actions today:

"Even as a solid rock is unshaken by the wind, so are the wise unshaken by praise or blame." - The Buddha

What is the measure of a person? How do we know if they are strong or weak? Often times, people are judged by how they react to others. When someone does something good, they are praised. When they do something wrong, they are frowned upon. Some people get so wrapped up in their success that when criticized, it takes an emotional toll on them. But what about the wise? The ones who know the difference between right and wrong?

Today's Date:

This quote inspires the following thoughts in me:

This quote inspires me to take these actions today:

(Before bedtime) I accomplished these actions today:

"People with opinions just go around bothering each other." - The Buddha

The world is full of people with opinions on just about everything, but what happens when these opinions clash? What do you do when someone's opinion of your life or your profession upsets you? You can't go to everyone with an opinion and tell them to shut up, even if it might feel great to do so. What instead?

Today's Date:

This quote inspires the following thoughts in me:

This quote inspires me to take these actions today:

(Before bedtime) I accomplished these actions today:

"When watching after yourself, you watch after others.
When watching after others, you watch after yourself."
- The Buddha

*When you offer support, encouragement, and kindness to others, it often turns
out that they are giving something back to you too. This is because empathy is
contagious - meaning that by caring for others around us, we are more likely to
feel compassionate toward ourselves.*

Today's Date:

This quote inspires the following thoughts in me:

This quote inspires me to take these actions today:

(Before bedtime) I accomplished these actions today:

"Silence the angry man with love. Silence the ill-natured man with kindness. Silence the miser with generosity. Silence the liar with truth." - The Buddha

Love is the most powerful tool in the world. It's what makes us humans so special, and helps us live our best lives. Love helps us stop being petty, point-scoring individuals and brings us together to offer support to one another. It can be used to silence an angry man, but it can also be used to help them find peace within themselves.

Today's Date:

This quote inspires the following thoughts in me:

This quote inspires me to take these actions today:

(Before bedtime) I accomplished these actions today:

"You, yourself, as much as anybody in the entire universe, deserve your love and affection."
- The Buddha

When you are feeling down, try to remember that you are worthy of love all the time. You have worth outside of what you produce or how well you perform in your relationships. You deserve to be loved for all of the things that make you who you are. There is no one else on the entire planet who deserves it more than you do. Do you find it hard to believe this?

Today's Date:

This quote inspires the following thoughts in me:

This quote inspires me to take these actions today:

(Before bedtime) I accomplished these actions today:

"Endurance is one of the most difficult disciplines, but it is to the one who endures that the final victory comes." - The Buddha

The hard work and determination it takes to stay committed to an endeavor for months or even years make it worth it in the end. The value of this victory is not lost on those who have suffered through the hardship. What are you working hard on? How do you keep going? From where do you draw your strength?

Today's Date:

This quote inspires the following thoughts in me:

This quote inspires me to take these actions today:

(Before bedtime) I accomplished these actions today:

"Like a fine flower, beautiful to look at but without scent, fine words are fruitless in a man who does not act in accordance with them." - The Buddha

Everyone has heard of the saying, "Actions speak louder than words." When it comes to the importance of integrity, this is especially true. If you say one thing but do another, you are not being honest with yourself or others. The more you ramble on about your honesty and integrity while never practicing what you preach, the more people will question your sincerity. Integrity can be summed up in just three words: Live Your Ideals.

Today's Date:

This quote inspires the following thoughts in me:

This quote inspires me to take these actions today:

(Before bedtime) I accomplished these actions today:

"Live every act fully, as if it were your last."
- The Buddha

Why does it feel so good to live life with abandon? When we have an experience, are we always aware that it's happening only once in a lifetime? Do we intuitively know that nothing ever lasts forever, or is that just a morbid thought that crosses into our consciousness every now and then when the timing seems right?

Today's Date:

This quote inspires the following thoughts in me:

This quote inspires me to take these actions today:

(Before bedtime) I accomplished these actions today:

"An insincere and evil friend is more to be feared than a wild beast; a wild beast may wound your body, but an evil friend will wound your mind."- The Buddha

Sometimes it's easy to tell when someone is your friend. They make you laugh, they make you feel cared for, and they share an interest in your life. Other times it can be difficult to know who your true friends are; you're afraid of offending them or confronting them because they might not like that. Often times people will say that a good friend is worth their weight in gold, but what if that friend wasn't good? What if they don't have your best interests in their heart? What are they worth then?

Today's Date:

This quote inspires the following thoughts in me:

This quote inspires me to take these actions today:

(Before bedtime) I accomplished these actions today:

"The root of suffering is attachment."
- The Buddha

The reason we experience pain and sorrow stems from a desire for things to be different than they are. Humans have a basic desire for happiness. We want to be happy and feel good as much as possible. Sometimes we pursue happiness in all the wrong ways and end up feeling miserable instead. The Buddha taught that people can rid themselves of suffering by learning to let go of attachments.

Today's Date:

This quote inspires the following thoughts in me:

This quote inspires me to take these actions today:

(Before bedtime) I accomplished these actions today:

"All that we are is the result of what we have thought."
- The Buddha

We tend to blame our circumstances for what we are. However, the truth is that we create our circumstances and we can change them. The Buddha said: "It is within your power" and "If you look at the world through the eyes of understanding, it will end all grief." What we think about becomes reality. Will that change how you think today, and what you think about today?

Today's Date:

This quote inspires the following thoughts in me:

This quote inspires me to take these actions today:

(Before bedtime) I accomplished these actions today:

"Radiate boundless love towards the entire world."
- The Buddha

Radiating boundless love towards the entire world may sound like an impossible, daunting task. But the truth is, it's not. It starts with one person to another. And then that person to another person. It starts with you and me. When we open our hearts to others by radiating our love outwards to them, they will do the same thing in return.

Today's Date:

This quote inspires the following thoughts in me:

This quote inspires me to take these actions today:

(Before bedtime) I accomplished these actions today:

"Ardently do today what must be done. Who knows?
Tomorrow, death comes." - The Buddha

Death is certain and unpredictable. Even the most humble and least educated people know this, but how many of us actually live like we believe it? It's almost as if we can get so used to living our lives in such a way that the idea of death becomes less scary than the idea of taking risks. What are you putting off for tomorrow, that really should be done today?

Today's Date:

This quote inspires the following thoughts in me:

This quote inspires me to take these actions today:

(Before bedtime) I accomplished these actions today:

"If we could see the miracle of a single flower clearly, our whole life would change." - The Buddha

We are often so busy with the hustle and bustle of life that we forget to stop, take a breath, and appreciate what is right in front of us. One beautiful flower can make all the difference because it reminds us to slow down, smell the roses, be grateful for what we have, and maybe even change our perspective on life.

Today's Date:

This quote inspires the following thoughts in me:

This quote inspires me to take these actions today:

(Before bedtime) I accomplished these actions today:

"Do not dwell in the past, do not dream of the future, concentrate the mind on the present moment."
- The Buddha

Remember to live in the moment. Breathe deeply, and let go of the past. Mindfulness is about living in the present, without judgement or regret. It is all too easy to dwell on things that have happened in the past - especially if they are negative experiences - or on things in the future, which may or may not come to us. The only moment we are actually alive is in this moment.

Today's Date:

This quote inspires the following thoughts in me:

This quote inspires me to take these actions today:

(Before bedtime) I accomplished these actions today:

"If with a pure mind a person speaks or acts happiness follows him like his never-departing shadow."
- The Buddha

Positive thoughts and actions create a positive atmosphere in which people can thrive. Conversely, negative thoughts and actions will cause stress and sadness to follow the individual who makes them. Are you proud of the shadow that follows you?

Today's Date:

This quote inspires the following thoughts in me:

This quote inspires me to take these actions today:

(Before bedtime) I accomplished these actions today:

"A man is not called wise because he talks and talks again; but if he is peaceful, loving and fearless then he is in truth called wise." - The Buddha

There are many different traits that people have, but to be considered wise, one must have three qualities: first, they must have knowledge of how to live their life wisely. Secondly, they must know how to live their life peacefully. Lastly, they must be fearless when it comes to doing the right thing. How many of these three can you confidently own in your life?

Today's Date:

This quote inspires the following thoughts in me:

This quote inspires me to take these actions today:

(Before bedtime) I accomplished these actions today:

"Everything that has a beginning has an ending. Make your peace with that and all will be well."
- The Buddha

It is a fact that we all need to accept: nothing lasts forever. Everything has a beginning and an end, and the end eventually comes. We should try to appreciate all the opportunities and successes we've had in life and spend our time doing meaningful things before it's too late!

Today's Date:

This quote inspires the following thoughts in me:

This quote inspires me to take these actions today:

(Before bedtime) I accomplished these actions today:

"Words have the power to both destroy and heal. When words are both true and kind, they can change our world." - The Buddha

When words are true and kind, they can change the world. What we say to others—especially those we love—can affect them deeply and last a lifetime. Who will you be talking to today? Do they need your kind and true words? Will you deny them your kind and true words?

Today's Date:

This quote inspires the following thoughts in me:

This quote inspires me to take these actions today:

(Before bedtime) I accomplished these actions today:

"Fashion your life as a garland of beautiful deeds."
- The Buddha

Many of us try to define ourselves by what we do for a living, the clothes we wear, the activities we engage in. But what if there was an alternative definition? What if one's life could be defined by their character and the good they have done?

Today's Date:

This quote inspires the following thoughts in me:

This quote inspires me to take these actions today:

(Before bedtime) I accomplished these actions today:

"Change is never painful. Only resistance to change is painful." - The Buddha

Change is a precursor to growth. It is a natural part of life that cannot be avoided. Be open to new opportunities. Imagine the amazing possibilities you may allow yourself by being willing to adapt to new circumstances as they come your way!

Today's Date:

This quote inspires the following thoughts in me:

This quote inspires me to take these actions today:

(Before bedtime) I accomplished these actions today:

"Holding onto anger is like drinking poison and expecting the other person to die." - The Buddha

Many of us hold onto anger for years, wondering why the other person or people who hurt us are still alive. We are often unaware that by holding on to anger, we are poisoning ourselves. What is our alternative? Telling the other person how angry they have made us by their behavior? Telling them to change their behavior so that they don't make us angry anymore? No. The only true way to free oneself from anger is to forgive. Are there people in your life you need to forgive? What are you waiting for?

Today's Date:

This quote inspires the following thoughts in me:

This quote inspires me to take these actions today:

(Before bedtime) I accomplished these actions today:

"True love is born from understanding." - The Buddha

Love is a word that is used in many cases. However, the truest love begins with understanding and compassion. A love that can withstand any hardship or tragedy because it has been built on a foundation of knowing and understanding each other's needs and desires - that is true love.

Today's Date:

This quote inspires the following thoughts in me:

This quote inspires me to take these actions today:

(Before bedtime) I accomplished these actions today:

"You don't meet people by accident. There is always a reason; a blessing or a lesson." - The Buddha

There is always a reason why we meet people. It could be that they are someone who will help us on our journey, or give us an important gift that teaches us something valuable. It's hard to know what's in store for us when you first meet someone but it's good to keep an open mind and pay attention for the lesson they might have to teach us.

Today's Date:

This quote inspires the following thoughts in me:

This quote inspires me to take these actions today:

(Before bedtime) I accomplished these actions today:

"A man who conquers himself is greater than one who conquers a thousand men in battle." - The Buddha

The length of one's life does not matter as much as the quality of that life. If you are able to conquer yourself and keep your spirit strong, you will be better off than someone who spends their entire life conquering others. What is it you need to conquer?

Today's Date:

This quote inspires the following thoughts in me:

This quote inspires me to take these actions today:

(Before bedtime) I accomplished these actions today:

"Don't carry your mistakes around with you. Instead, place them under your feet and use them as stepping stones." - The Buddha

The phrase "carry your mistakes around with you" depicts remorseful individuals, dragging the weight of their past actions behind them. However, there is another way to view these same actions. Every time we make a mistake, we take an important step. These steps may not be the ones we expected or hoped for, but they are still steps in the right direction - regardless of how hopeless they may seem.

Today's Date:

This quote inspires the following thoughts in me:

This quote inspires me to take these actions today:

(Before bedtime) I accomplished these actions today:

"One tree makes millions of match sticks. Only one match stick needs to burn millions of trees. So be good and do good." - The Buddha

Are you the tree or the matchstick? Which do you want to be? A single kindness may yield many kindnesses; an unkindness may hurt you and many others and yield other unkindnesses. Of course you know which is better. How many matchsticks will you create today?

Today's Date:

This quote inspires the following thoughts in me:

This quote inspires me to take these actions today:

(Before bedtime) I accomplished these actions today:

"Life is uncertain; death is certain." - The Buddha

We are born with no idea of how long we will live. It is something that has always been uncertain to us. This uncertainty only increases the closer you get to death. For some people, this isn't a big deal because they have lived their life with courage and bravery. For others, they might want to take steps to prepare for their demise. What have you done to face your death fearlessly?

Today's Date:

This quote inspires the following thoughts in me:

This quote inspires me to take these actions today:

(Before bedtime) I accomplished these actions today:

"No one outside ourselves can rule us inwardly. When we know this, we become free." - The Buddha

The only person who can rule over our inner thoughts and feelings is ourselves. The more we know this, the more free we will be from external pressures. We typically feel that society dictates how we should perceive ourselves and behave in certain situations, but when we realize that no one outside of us will ever truly rule what is going on inside of us, it is liberating.

Today's Date:

This quote inspires the following thoughts in me:

This quote inspires me to take these actions today:

(Before bedtime) I accomplished these actions today:

"When wishes are few, the heart is happy. When craving ends, there is peace." - The Buddha

Today, in a world where we have access to all of our desires at a click of a button, it can be hard to find peace. But in reality, when you look for peace in all the wrong places, you've been looking in the wrong directions. Look within. Peace is so close you can feel it.

Today's Date:

This quote inspires the following thoughts in me:

This quote inspires me to take these actions today:

(Before bedtime) I accomplished these actions today:

"Just as a snake sheds it's skin, we must shed our past over and over again." - The Buddha

We all have a past. Some things we look back on and regret, others we might be proud of. Regardless of what our past entails, we can learn to be stronger and better than ever before because of the choices we made in the past. The past is just that-past. Let it go. It doesn't define us or dictate who we can be.

Today's Date:

This quote inspires the following thoughts in me:

This quote inspires me to take these actions today:

(Before bedtime) I accomplished these actions today:

"Your worst enemy is your best teacher."
- The Buddha

The worst moments in life are the most important, because they shape you. These moments are not necessarily bad - they can be ones that end up saving your life. Think back on your life. What events have had a profound effect on you? What events have shaped you into the person you are today?

Today's Date:

This quote inspires the following thoughts in me:

This quote inspires me to take these actions today:

(Before bedtime) I accomplished these actions today:

"Assumptions are the termites of relationships."
- The Buddha

Assumptions may start small and unnoticeable, but they gradually eat away at our structure until it crumbles. Our friends, family members, and romantic partners love us for who we are - not because of assumptions made about who they think we are. Are there terminates in your foundation?

Today's Date:

This quote inspires the following thoughts in me:

This quote inspires me to take these actions today:

(Before bedtime) I accomplished these actions today:

"If your compassion does not include yourself, it is incomplete." - The Buddha

Compassionate people are aware of their own needs and wants in order to be sensitive to the needs of others. It's important for compassionate people to take care of themselves in order to take care of others. Do you take good enough care of your self? How can you be at your best for others if you are not at your best for yourself?

Today's Date:

This quote inspires the following thoughts in me:

This quote inspires me to take these actions today:

(Before bedtime) I accomplished these actions today:

"Those who cling to perceptions and views wander the world offending people." - The Buddha

Much like a toddler throwing a tantrum, those who cling to perceptions and views often offend those they come in contact with as they make their way through life. They can be found turning up their noses at the world around them and judging those who don't think the same way as them. But this mode of thought does not lead to freedom and peace; instead, it leaves us burdened and aggravated, frustrated by the world and those we encounter on our path.

Today's Date:

This quote inspires the following thoughts in me:

This quote inspires me to take these actions today:

(Before bedtime) I accomplished these actions today:

"One who acts on truth is happy in this world and beyond." - The Buddha

Am I always at peace with myself and my surroundings? I never worry about the outcome of my actions, because I know that if my intentions are true, everything usually works out in the end. No matter how much time and effort I spend on a project, I am happy to do so because it will not be in vain. The people who come into contact with me will be changed for the better and become more humane. Is this something you can tell yourself honestly?

Today's Date:

This quote inspires the following thoughts in me:

This quote inspires me to take these actions today:

(Before bedtime) I accomplished these actions today:

"If you propose to speak always ask yourself, is it true, is it necessary, is it kind?" - The Buddha

When we speak out, we often don't give much thought to the consequences that our words may have. It's important to keep in mind that when we say something it can often be taken in a way that was never originally intended. Sometimes the wisest approach is to say nothing at all.

Today's Date:

This quote inspires the following thoughts in me:

This quote inspires me to take these actions today:

(Before bedtime) I accomplished these actions today:

"Every human being is the author of his own health or disease." - The Buddha

We all have the power to create our own reality, including the physical one. Our thoughts are what leads to change in our lives, including in our physical state. The key is to think positively and feel great about yourself in order to lead a healthy lifestyle. If you can believe in your self-worth and keep a positive mind set, you will be much more likely to achieve good health.

Today's Date:

This quote inspires the following thoughts in me:

This quote inspires me to take these actions today:

(Before bedtime) I accomplished these actions today:

"Develop and cultivate the liberation of mind by loving-kindness, make it our vehicle, make it our basis, stabilize it, exercise ourselves in it, and fully perfect it." - The Buddha

Loving-kindness is the only way to serve all beings. It's a universal law that is dependable and can be cultivated to make everyone free from suffering. Loving-kindness thrives when it follows these principles. How many do you incorporate into your life each day?

Today's Date:

This quote inspires the following thoughts in me:

This quote inspires me to take these actions today:

(Before bedtime) I accomplished these actions today:

"He is able who thinks he is able."
- The Buddha

The old proverb "He who thinks he can, and he who thinks he cannot, are both right" is so true. He who has the power to believe in himself, will always find a way to get what he wants. Is there something you want to bring into the universe? Do you think you can? Do you know that you can?

Today's Date:

This quote inspires the following thoughts in me:

This quote inspires me to take these actions today:

(Before bedtime) I accomplished these actions today:

"Transcendental intelligence rises when the intellectual mind reaches its limit and if things are to be realized in their true and essential nature, its processes of thinking must be transcended by an appeal to some higher faculty of cognition." - The Buddha

Transcendental intelligence is the innate capacity of our minds to comprehend things that are beyond our thinking processes, somewhat like being able to intuitively understand this quote without any mental effort!

Today's Date:

This quote inspires the following thoughts in me:

This quote inspires me to take these actions today:

(Before bedtime) I accomplished these actions today:

"Should a person do good, let him do it again and again. Let him find pleasure therein, for blissful is the accumulation of good." - The Buddha

People who do good deeds and encourage others to do the same, can find great happiness in this world and in the hereafter. A person's good deeds should be nurtured and encouraged with kindness for it is a blessing. The most powerful motivator for good deeds is kindness. It's not enough for you to do good deeds. You must also encourage others to do the same.

Today's Date:

This quote inspires the following thoughts in me:

This quote inspires me to take these actions today:

(Before bedtime) I accomplished these actions today:

"The past is already gone, the future is not yet here. There's only one moment for you to live." - The Buddha

We often find ourselves thinking of moments that have passed or worrying about what will happen in the future, but we forget that there is only one moment for us to live in. The time after this moment will be gone before we know it and our future worries are too far away to even imagine; all we have left is this present moment.

Today's Date:

This quote inspires the following thoughts in me:

This quote inspires me to take these actions today:

(Before bedtime) I accomplished these actions today:

"Don't rush anything. When the time is right, it'll happen." - The Buddha

Sometimes life only presents us with more questions and what seems like dead ends. That's when we need to let go of expectations and stay open for whatever the next step might be. Meditate. Breathe. Let go. The answers will come.

Today's Date:

This quote inspires the following thoughts in me:

This quote inspires me to take these actions today:

(Before bedtime) I accomplished these actions today:

"If you do not change direction, you may end up where you are heading." - The Buddha

We often find ourselves in a rut. One day, we're up and the next day, we're down. Sometimes it feels like we're stuck in the same place, doing the same thing over and over. These are common signs of what's called an existential crisis. Let go of the existential crisis. It doesn't actually exist. Your true compass is within you, and will not lead you astray.

Today's Date:

This quote inspires the following thoughts in me:

This quote inspires me to take these actions today:

(Before bedtime) I accomplished these actions today:

"On life's journey faith is nourishment, virtuous deeds are a shelter, wisdom is the light by day and right mindfulness is the protection by night. If a man lives a pure life, nothing can destroy him." - The Buddha

How we can live a more virtuous life in order to avoid the significant damage we inflict upon ourselves when we make bad decisions? Living a virtuous life not only benefits us but also those around us and furthers our journey through life.

Today's Date:

This quote inspires the following thoughts in me:

This quote inspires me to take these actions today:

(Before bedtime) I accomplished these actions today:

"Life is dear to all beings, they have the right to live the same that we do." - The Buddha

Life is a fragile and precious thing and every living being should be afforded the right to live it. There are many different animals that deserve this same right, not just us humans. We need to stop letting ourselves think we're at the top of the food chain and start recognizing that we're all interdependent with each other in some way.

Today's Date:

This quote inspires the following thoughts in me:

This quote inspires me to take these actions today:

(Before bedtime) I accomplished these actions today:

"Anger will never disappear so long as thoughts of resentment are cherished in the mind. Anger will disappear just as soon as thoughts of resentment are forgotten." - The Buddha

Anger is an emotion that seeks to inflate itself, through condemning other individuals or objects, often without any evidence to back up this condemnation. It's important to remember that anger is a natural part of life, but we should strive to live without it all the time. Like all negative things, you have the power to let it go if you choose to. Will you?

Today's Date:

This quote inspires the following thoughts in me:

This quote inspires me to take these actions today:

(Before bedtime) I accomplished these actions today:

"The world is a looking glass. It gives back to every man a true reflection of his own thoughts. Rule your mind or it will rule you." - The Buddha

No one in the world is perfect. Every day we create and commit to actions that we would be better off not doing. When we do these things, our actions become reflections of what's in our heads and what we want for ourselves. But just as our appearance changes from day to day, so can our thoughts and actions. Strive always to be better today than you were yesterday.

Today's Date:

This quote inspires the following thoughts in me:

This quote inspires me to take these actions today:

(Before bedtime) I accomplished these actions today:

"Remembering a wrong is like carrying a burden on the mind." - The Buddha

It is important to remember that when someone wrongs you, they do not make you a victim. Instead, they simply give you an opportunity to show the world what you are capable of and how much more resilient and resourceful you can be. When we cling to negativity we carry it on our minds and in turn burden ourselves with the weight of it all. It is important to forgive.

Today's Date:

This quote inspires the following thoughts in me:

This quote inspires me to take these actions today:

(Before bedtime) I accomplished these actions today:

"It is better to walk alone than with a crowd going in the wrong direction." - The Buddha

When it comes to decision-making, people often feel more compelled by the opinions of others and less inclined to explore their own thoughts and beliefs. This leaves them vulnerable to being manipulated by other's ideas. One way to avoid this is to take time for solitude, self-reflection, and contemplation. Find your own path. Follow your own drummer. This is the only way for you to discover peace.

Today's Date:

This quote inspires the following thoughts in me:

This quote inspires me to take these actions today:

(Before bedtime) I accomplished these actions today:

"When you like a flower, you just pluck it. But when you love a flower, you water it daily." - The Buddha

Everything we love is a result of cultivation. The plants that grow in our gardens, the words we use to express ourselves, and even our relationships with others are all cultivated to some extent. For many people, the best way to nurture something they love is by simply focusing on it. What will you water today? What will you merely pluck?

Today's Date:

This quote inspires the following thoughts in me:

This quote inspires me to take these actions today:

(Before bedtime) I accomplished these actions today:

"In separateness lies the world's greatest misery; in compassion lies the world's true strength."
- The Buddha

We are all connected. When we think we are separate from each other, we become miserable. But together in compassion, we are strong. We all suffer when someone else is suffering. Our happiness can't be confined to ourselves, no matter how much love for ourselves we have. If I am joyful, it's because someone else allowed me to feel that way. Share it all.

Today's Date:

This quote inspires the following thoughts in me:

This quote inspires me to take these actions today:

(Before bedtime) I accomplished these actions today:

77

"Happiness comes when your work and words are of benefit to yourself and others." - The Buddha

It is often said that happiness comes from being a servant, not a master. This means that service to others creates a sense of fulfillment and contentment with life. In order to be happy, one must find a way to serve themselves and the lives of others. It's important to know when you are in need of help or if you can offer help to those in need as well as those who don't realize they need it.

Today's Date:

This quote inspires the following thoughts in me:

This quote inspires me to take these actions today:

(Before bedtime) I accomplished these actions today:

"Forget the past that makes you cry and focus on the present that makes you smile." - The Buddha

Life can be tough when you have a lot going on in your head. It becomes a balancing act between mental and physical health, past demons, and future goals. But what if we could stop worrying about the past that makes you cry and focus on the present that makes you smile? What if we could take each day as it comes? Let it go.

Today's Date:

This quote inspires the following thoughts in me:

This quote inspires me to take these actions today:

(Before bedtime) I accomplished these actions today:

"It is ridiculous to think that somebody else can make you happy or unhappy." - The Buddha

You are the only one who gets to decide whether happiness is an option for your life, so don't waste any more time blaming others for your unhappiness. Start accepting responsibility for your own happiness and watch happiness flow to you!

Today's Date:

This quote inspires the following thoughts in me:

This quote inspires me to take these actions today:

(Before bedtime) I accomplished these actions today:

"Arguing with stupid people is like trying to kill the mosquito on your cheek. You may or may not kill it, but you will in any event slap yourself." - The Buddha

Arguing with someone is a futile, time-consuming endeavor that many of us have been drawn into on more than one occasion. We may feel compelled to argue because we believe the other person is wrong, they're driving us crazy or simply because they're an obstinate person who will not relent. Is there a better way? Do you always have to "win"?

Today's Date:

This quote inspires the following thoughts in me:

This quote inspires me to take these actions today:

(Before bedtime) I accomplished these actions today:

"Judge nothing, you will be happy. Forgive everything, you will be happier. Love everything, you will be happiest." - The Buddha

Far too often, we judge our experiences and the people around us based on what we think they should be. We justify our own unhappiness because of external factors, but in reality, it is the way we choose to respond to those external factors that make us happy or unhappy. It's important to not only forgive those who have wronged us, but also understand that we can experience happiness even through suffering.

Today's Date:

This quote inspires the following thoughts in me:

This quote inspires me to take these actions today:

(Before bedtime) I accomplished these actions today:

"Don't devalue or hurt anyone in life. You may be powerful today. But remember, time is more powerful than you." - The Buddha

There is nothing more powerful in life than time. It can help us move forward or it can make us feel stuck in the past with painful memories. When we devalue others in our lives, we are doing ourselves a disservice because not only are they hurting, but so are we.

Today's Date:

This quote inspires the following thoughts in me:

This quote inspires me to take these actions today:

(Before bedtime) I accomplished these actions today:

"Do not be sad, the end is near, but life is ever-changing." - The Buddha

Our lives are just moments, and it is important that we seize these moments to create an existence full of love. It is simple that the world needs us all to live fully now, so be brave and do not give up. Be strong and keep going forward.

Today's Date:

This quote inspires the following thoughts in me:

This quote inspires me to take these actions today:

(Before bedtime) I accomplished these actions today:

"To be idle is a short road to death and to be diligent is a way of life; foolish people are idle, wise people are diligent." - The Buddha

It is important to be diligent in order to have a fulfilling life. People who are not diligent don't have anything going on in their lives to keep them motivated or satisfied. This can lead to feelings of emptiness and unhappiness that they may not be able to overcome. What are the areas of your life that you could be more diligent about?

Today's Date:

This quote inspires the following thoughts in me:

This quote inspires me to take these actions today:

(Before bedtime) I accomplished these actions today:

"Do not give your attention to what others do or failed to do; give it to what you do or failed to do."
- The Buddha

It can be very eye opening to take a step back and evaluate your life. What have you done so far? What have you failed to do? We need to focus on our own life, because we are the only ones who truly know what we want out of it. Other people's choices and decisions should not affect the quality of ours.

Today's Date:

This quote inspires the following thoughts in me:

This quote inspires me to take these actions today:

(Before bedtime) I accomplished these actions today:

"To stop suffering, stop greediness. Greediness is a source of suffering." - The Buddha

It's a human tendency to cling tightly onto certain things with the hope that they will provide us with happiness. When we hold on too tightly, it can cause us to suffer because what we're clinging to may eventually escape our grasp due to circumstances outside of our control. By letting go, we are at peace knowing that it's not up to us to control what's going on in the world around us.

Today's Date:

This quote inspires the following thoughts in me:

This quote inspires me to take these actions today:

(Before bedtime) I accomplished these actions today:

"Serenity comes when you trade expectations for acceptance." - The Buddha

In our pursuit to make life perfect, we often set expectations for ourselves which are impossible to meet. We then find ourselves feeling disappointed and let down when we inevitably fail to meet them. It's a vicious cycle that leads to a lack of contentment and peace. When we come to terms with the fact that "perfection" doesn't exist, it becomes easier to be content with what we have and where we are.

Today's Date:

This quote inspires the following thoughts in me:

This quote inspires me to take these actions today:

(Before bedtime) I accomplished these actions today:

"If you are poor, live wisely. If you are rich, live wisely. It is not your station in life but your heart that brings blessings." - The Buddha

It is often said that there are two ways to live your life: rich and poor. While the world strives for more wealth, it would be wise to also strive for wisdom. With or without money, there are many lessons that can be learned in order to live a fulfilled life. There's nothing wrong with earning a good living, especially if you are able to share the fruit of your labors.

Today's Date:

This quote inspires the following thoughts in me:

This quote inspires me to take these actions today:

(Before bedtime) I accomplished these actions today:

"A lovely thing to learn from water: Adjust yourself in every situation and in any shape. But most importantly. Find your own way to flow."
- The Buddha

Water is something that should be imitated in every aspect of life. Water can adjust to any situation and any shape. It never gives up, it never stops, and it always finds its way to flow. This can be seen in the physical fluidity of water or in the spiritual sense of staying true to oneself no matter what. When you feel like you are fighting an uphill battle, remember what water does and emulate this trait!

Today's Date:

This quote inspires the following thoughts in me:

This quote inspires me to take these actions today:

(Before bedtime) I accomplished these actions today:

"A true relationship is when you can tell each other anything and everything. No secrets, no lies."
- The Buddha

The key to a successful relationship is being able to tell each other everything and anything without fear of judgement or disapproval. Secrets and lies cheat the other person out of what they deserve; the ability to make their own choices and determine their own future.

Today's Date:

This quote inspires the following thoughts in me:

This quote inspires me to take these actions today:

(Before bedtime) I accomplished these actions today:

"Release old concepts and energies that keep you in self-punishment patterns. Release old stories and create from a place of love and self-validation. You are worth it!" - The Buddha

We are always trying to change, but so many times we are stuck in the same patterns. Imagine what it would feel like to release all the patterns of self-punishment that keep you stuck in a loop of negativity. Give it shot. Let it go. You can do this, right?

Today's Date:

This quote inspires the following thoughts in me:

This quote inspires me to take these actions today:

(Before bedtime) I accomplished these actions today:

"Should you find a wise critic to point out your faults, follow him as you would a guide to hidden treasure."
- The Buddha

There are many benefits that come from having a critic point out your faults. They can point out things you don't notice on your own and help you to grow as a person. A good critic will critique aspects of your life, not just work or art. A wise critic will also provide positive feedback on the positives of one's life too. The best critics are those who teach lessons through their criticism. A great teacher knows how to provide criticism without breaking the student down.

Today's Date:

This quote inspires the following thoughts in me:

This quote inspires me to take these actions today:

(Before bedtime) I accomplished these actions today:

"Do not look for a sanctuary in anyone except your self."
- The Buddha

Your sanctuary is the space you inhabit, the company you keep. It is not in anyone else's hands or on anyone else's time. You do not need to look for it in them; it will be found only in yourself. Your sanctuary is the knowledge that no matter what happens, no matter what others do, if you can find your way back home to this space within yourself, there will be peace.

Today's Date:

This quote inspires the following thoughts in me:

This quote inspires me to take these actions today:

(Before bedtime) I accomplished these actions today:

"Ambition is like love, impatient both of delays and rivals." - The Buddha

It will not be wooed nor will it wait; it is not concerned with the head or heart, but wants only his desire and nothing else matters. Strive on and achieve your goals, but be wise and patient allow the way to achieving them.

Today's Date:

This quote inspires the following thoughts in me:

This quote inspires me to take these actions today:

(Before bedtime) I accomplished these actions today:

"Our life is shaped by our mind; we become what we think. Joy follows a pure thought like a shadow that never leaves." - The Buddha

One moment of joy can make all the pain worth it. Even in the depths of despair, joy can be found with only a single thought or image of happiness. The power of our thoughts and emotions is extraordinary and affects not only ourselves, but also those around us.

Today's Date:

This quote inspires the following thoughts in me:

This quote inspires me to take these actions today:

(Before bedtime) I accomplished these actions today:

"Let all-embracing thoughts for all beings be yours."
- The Buddha

The peace of mind and safety of all beings is a goal so great that it is worth striving for, no matter what the cost. But it can be difficult to spread benevolence broadly. What if we start with ourselves? What if, every day, we were to cultivate love and compassion for ourselves, first and foremost?

Today's Date:

This quote inspires the following thoughts in me:

This quote inspires me to take these actions today:

(Before bedtime) I accomplished these actions today:

"Everything is based on mind, is led by mind, is fashioned by mind. If you speak and act with a polluted mind, suffering will follow you, as the wheels of the oxcart follow the footsteps of the ox."
- The Buddha

We are all aware of how our actions and thoughts affect our lives. When we act on what is pure in mind, we lead a more fulfilled life. If we act with polluted thoughts, then it follows that suffering will come to us. But by acting with pure thoughts, not only will the world be happier but so will you.

Today's Date:

This quote inspires the following thoughts in me:

This quote inspires me to take these actions today:

(Before bedtime) I accomplished these actions today:

"Thousands of candles can be lighted from a single candle, and the life of the candle will not be shortened. Happiness never decreases by being shared."
- The Buddha

Why is it that some of us find it easier to ignore the pain of others rather than offer a comforting word, or provide some sort of service? Happiness can increase when shared with others, so it makes sense to share your happiness, and relieve the pain of others. Whom do you know who needs your comfort today?

Today's Date:

This quote inspires the following thoughts in me:

This quote inspires me to take these actions today:

(Before bedtime) I accomplished these actions today:

"Do not turn away what is given you, nor reach out for what is given to others, lest you disturb your quietness." - The Buddha

One should accept with gratitude any opportunities or goods that are given by someone else. This should be done without seeking out more than what is rightfully owed to them according to the situation.

Today's Date:

This quote inspires the following thoughts in me:

This quote inspires me to take these actions today:

(Before bedtime) I accomplished these actions today:

"There are only two mistakes one can make along the road to truth; not going all the way, and not starting."
- The Buddha

The journey of discovery is not without its obstacles. The first is not to go on the journey at all. The second is to start, but never finish. However, there is no reward without risk and mastery requires practice. It may feel like you are crawling up an insurmountable mountain, but in reality you are climbing a ladder that will help you reach your goals.

Today's Date:

This quote inspires the following thoughts in me:

This quote inspires me to take these actions today:

(Before bedtime) I accomplished these actions today:

"Be where you are; otherwise you will miss your life."
- The Buddha

We all have the tendency to want what we're not. We are always chasing an experience, feeling, state of mind, or mindset that is just out of our reach. When you are content with where you are, you feel accomplished and satisfied. But when you are comparing yourself to where you wish you were, it leaves a void of incompleteness.

Today's Date:

This quote inspires the following thoughts in me:

This quote inspires me to take these actions today:

(Before bedtime) I accomplished these actions today:

"Be truthful; do not yield to anger. Give freely, even if you have but little." - The Buddha

When someone else irritates us with their actions, instead of responding in anger, we should respond kindly. This will show them that we care about them and that they are valued in our eyes. Give to others without expecting anything in return; it is an act of kindness that should never go unrealized.

Today's Date:

This quote inspires the following thoughts in me:

This quote inspires me to take these actions today:

(Before bedtime) I accomplished these actions today:

"Better it is to live one day seeing the rise and fall of things than to live a hundred years without ever seeing the rise and fall of things." - The Buddha

Many people believe that it is better to live a long and boring life than to experience new and exciting things. These people often go through their days with little excitement and accomplishment. Life is not meant to be mundane and safe, sometimes we need to take risks in order to experience the full range of emotions that life has to offer.

Today's Date:

This quote inspires the following thoughts in me:

This quote inspires me to take these actions today:

(Before bedtime) I accomplished these actions today:

"Every morning is a symbol of rebirth of our life, so forget all yesterday's bad moments and make today the most beautiful day of your life." - The Buddha

Every morning you wake up, your life is renewed. All the bad moments of yesterday are forgotten and all new possibilities for today are in front of you waiting to be discovered. Take the time to cherish this moment and make it the best day of your life.

Today's Date:

This quote inspires the following thoughts in me:

This quote inspires me to take these actions today:

(Before bedtime) I accomplished these actions today:

"Don't compare yourself with anyone in this world. If you do so, you're insulting yourself." - The Buddha

Stop comparing yourself with others and start accepting yourself for who you are. You are one-of-a-kind so embrace what makes you different from everyone else because it'll make you happy!

Today's Date:

This quote inspires the following thoughts in me:

This quote inspires me to take these actions today:

(Before bedtime) I accomplished these actions today:

"Since everything is a reflection of our minds, everything can be changed by our minds."
- The Buddha

We all know that we must eat well and take care of our bodies, but what we don't realize is that we also need to do the same for our minds. Our minds can be changed by what we think about and what we feed them. If you want to change the way you see things, you have to change your thoughts. What you focus on is important because this will determine what you'll experience in your life.

Today's Date:

This quote inspires the following thoughts in me:

This quote inspires me to take these actions today:

(Before bedtime) I accomplished these actions today:

"Care about what other people think and you will always be their prisoner." - The Buddha

It's easy to get distracted by the opinions of other people. They sway us into thinking that our decisions are wrong or that we're not good enough. Living in a world where everyone has an opinion, it feels like there is no escape from them. But can you care about what other people think? Should you? What are the consequences of caring too much about what people think? It's time to break free from the opinions of others and start living for yourself.

Today's Date:

This quote inspires the following thoughts in me:

This quote inspires me to take these actions today:

(Before bedtime) I accomplished these actions today:

"Love is a gift of one's innermost soul to another so both can be whole." - The Buddha

There are many different types of love and it takes many forms, but they all share one thing in common: they bring us closer to wholeness. All types of love draw on our deepest emotions and most primal instincts and we need all types of love to create balance in our lives.

Today's Date:

This quote inspires the following thoughts in me:

This quote inspires me to take these actions today:

(Before bedtime) I accomplished these actions today:

"Always love your friends from your heart and not from your needs." - The Buddha

The need to please friends has a tendency of making people fake their feelings and keep up with the fake self they have created. It is important to know when you need to stop putting your friends before yourself and make the decision that is best for you.

Today's Date:

This quote inspires the following thoughts in me:

This quote inspires me to take these actions today:

(Before bedtime) I accomplished these actions today:

"When you realize how perfect everything is you will tilt your head back and laugh at the sky."
- The Buddha

The way that life unfolds in front of us is natural and beautiful, and it's important to embrace it for what it is - a perfect story filled with all manner of experiences that we get to write together with our family, friends, and loved ones.

Today's Date:

This quote inspires the following thoughts in me:

This quote inspires me to take these actions today:

(Before bedtime) I accomplished these actions today:

"Don't think too much. Just do what makes you happy."
- The Buddha

Deep in our being, there is a voice that whispers to us in moments of doubt. It tells us to be true to ourselves and do what makes us happy. For when we follow this voice, it will lead us to the joys of life. When we don't listen, it can leave us feeling emptied out. What do you hear?

Today's Date:

This quote inspires the following thoughts in me:

This quote inspires me to take these actions today:

(Before bedtime) I accomplished these actions today:

"Holding on to anger is like grasping a hot coal with the intent of throwing it at someone else; you are the one who gets burned." - The Buddha

We all know that holding onto anger is an unhealthy way to live. We are the ones who are the most injured by our own bitterness. But what is it about anger that makes us so difficult to let go of? Why do we have such a hard time managing our feelings after being wronged?

Today's Date:

This quote inspires the following thoughts in me:

This quote inspires me to take these actions today:

(Before bedtime) I accomplished these actions today:

"Forgive those who insult you, attack you, belittle you or take you for granted. But more than this ... forgive yourself for allowing them to hurt you." - The Buddha

It's never easy to forgive someone for hurting us, but in order to move on with our lives, we need to let go of the negative feelings associated with the situation. But more than this, forgive yourself for allowing them to hurt you. The wounds inflicted by others will not heal until we realize that they can only hurt us if we give them permission to.

Today's Date:

This quote inspires the following thoughts in me:

This quote inspires me to take these actions today:

(Before bedtime) I accomplished these actions today:

"He who causes suffering shall suffer. There is no escape." - The Buddha

The idea of karma is rooted in the law of cause and effect: actions create reactions. It can be hard to see how this principle applies to our daily lives at first glance. But if we commit negative acts will we experience negativity in return, perhaps not immediately, but as surely as the sun rises.

Today's Date:

This quote inspires the following thoughts in me:

This quote inspires me to take these actions today:

(Before bedtime) I accomplished these actions today:

"No one can escape death and unhappiness. If people expect only happiness in life, they will be disappointed." - The Buddha

One must face unhappiness and the knowledge of death in order to live a complete life, despite what people might have been led to believe. There are many aspects of life that one needs to experience before they can truly understand what it means to be alive.

Today's Date:

This quote inspires the following thoughts in me:

This quote inspires me to take these actions today:

(Before bedtime) I accomplished these actions today:

"Do not learn how to react. Learn how to respond."
- The Buddha

We can all learn how to respond to all situations with compassion. It's important because it allows the person we're interacting with to feel valued and respected, which is better for them and lessens stress on us. With a little practice, it makes it much easier to be compassionate in every situation.

Today's Date:

This quote inspires the following thoughts in me:

This quote inspires me to take these actions today:

(Before bedtime) I accomplished these actions today:

"The wind cannot overturn a mountain. Temptation cannot touch the man who is awake, strong and humble."- The Buddha

In order to be safe from temptation, you must stay rooted in your beliefs and not stray from what you know to be right or wrong. Are you as strong as a mountain?

Today's Date:

This quote inspires the following thoughts in me:

This quote inspires me to take these actions today:

(Before bedtime) I accomplished these actions today:

"Go easy on yourself. Whatever you do today, let it be enough." - The Buddha

Self-love and self-care are often lost in the rat race of everyday life. We're too busy trying to do more and be better than we ever have before to stop and really think about what is going on with ourselves. It's important to remember that there is no harm in slowing down to take time for yourself, so whatever you do today, let it be enough.

Today's Date:

This quote inspires the following thoughts in me:

This quote inspires me to take these actions today:

(Before bedtime) I accomplished these actions today:

"Awake. Be the witness of your thoughts. You are what observes, not what you observe." - The Buddha

Why are you not awake? What are you waiting for? Your heart is pumping, your lungs take in and release air. The universe is alive with vibrant energies. But still, you lay there and do nothing. Wake up! You have a chance to take in the world and see it all. Every detail in every possible view and every possible angle. There is no way to miss it. If you're awake, then you're always watching the show that never ends.

Today's Date:

This quote inspires the following thoughts in me:

This quote inspires me to take these actions today:

(Before bedtime) I accomplished these actions today:

"Make truth your island, make truth your refuge; there is no other refuge." - The Buddha

Truth remains the only refuge for those seeking to escape that which would otherwise destroy them. The cost of a life without truth, and that which it demands, will be devastating.

Today's Date:

This quote inspires the following thoughts in me:

This quote inspires me to take these actions today:

(Before bedtime) I accomplished these actions today:

"At the bottom of things, most people want to be understood and appreciated." - The Buddha

But how do we make sense of this? How does understanding and appreciation work in the complex world we live in today? To answer these questions, it is important to understand what the need for understanding and appreciation is for: it gives us a sense of belonging and worthiness that is essential to human functioning. To receive it, you should first give it, in abundance. Do you?

Today's Date:

This quote inspires the following thoughts in me:

This quote inspires me to take these actions today:

(Before bedtime) I accomplished these actions today:

"Whoever doesn't flare up at someone who's angry wins a battle hard to win." - The Buddha

Stay calm and compassionate, and your foe will be embarrassed for getting so worked up in the first place. The anger is likely a projection of their own insecurity and fear, and once you stand firm yet speak peace, they will eventually see themselves as they are, and see you for what you are.

Today's Date:

This quote inspires the following thoughts in me:

This quote inspires me to take these actions today:

(Before bedtime) I accomplished these actions today:

"What you are is what you have been. What you'll be is what you do now." - The Buddha

Are you what you have been? Is there anything more reliable to determine your identity than the place you are now, the things you have now, the people around you now?

Today's Date:

This quote inspires the following thoughts in me:

This quote inspires me to take these actions today:

(Before bedtime) I accomplished these actions today:

"Whatever precious jewel there is in the heavenly worlds, there is nothing comparable to one who is Awakened." - The Buddha

The experience of life is an incredible journey. The ability to be aware and fully conscious in this moment, and not get caught up in the past or the future is more valuable than any jewel that comes from the ground.

Today's Date:

This quote inspires the following thoughts in me:

This quote inspires me to take these actions today:

(Before bedtime) I accomplished these actions today:

"Whatever words we utter should be chosen with care for people will hear them and be influenced by them for good or ill." - The Buddha

Think of the words you use to speak to your children, friends, coworkers, and even strangers. The words you use can either uplift or tear down another person's self esteem. You never know what someone is going through; always offer words of kindness and compassion. You will never go wrong.

Today's Date:

This quote inspires the following thoughts in me:

This quote inspires me to take these actions today:

(Before bedtime) I accomplished these actions today:

"All experiences are preceded by mind, having mind as their master, created by mind." - The Buddha

It doesn't matter what it is you are doing or where you are, your experience of it is shaped by your thoughts. Knowing this, how will you actively shape your experience of the world today?

Today's Date:

This quote inspires the following thoughts in me:

This quote inspires me to take these actions today:

(Before bedtime) I accomplished these actions today:

"Looking deeply at life as it is in this very moment, the meditator dwells in stability and freedom."
- The Buddha

It's time to break free of the patterns that we've been repeating and always living in. It's time to go beyond the surface and truly see what is happening: our thoughts, feelings, and sensations. When we live in this way, we can experience a sense of stability and freedom.

Today's Date:

This quote inspires the following thoughts in me:

This quote inspires me to take these actions today:

(Before bedtime) I accomplished these actions today:

"In the end, only three things matters: how much you loved, how gently you lived, and how gracefully you let go of things not meant for you." - The Buddha

We often think of these three things as separate, but they are intertwined in one continuous loop. One cannot be loved without living gently and letting go. And one cannot live gently without loving and letting go. These three things are essentially inseparable because they define each other.

Today's Date:

This quote inspires the following thoughts in me:

This quote inspires me to take these actions today:

(Before bedtime) I accomplished these actions today:

"Leave behind confused reactions and become patient as the earth; unmoved by anger, unshaken as a pillar, unperturbed as a clear and quiet pool." - The Buddha

Sometimes we get caught up in the whirlwind of emotions that sweep over our mind and body. It is only natural that we would be confused and uncertain about what to do, but it is important to remember that reactions like this will not help you get through your challenging situation. Stay calm, and project compassion.

Today's Date:

This quote inspires the following thoughts in me:

This quote inspires me to take these actions today:

(Before bedtime) I accomplished these actions today:

"It seems that although we thought ourselves permanent, we are not. Although we thought ourselves settled, we are not. Although we thought we would last forever, we will not." - The Buddha

We are temporary beings and we live with the illusion that we are permanent and settled. Yet we cannot escape death and we will not last forever. We all die and many things crumble with time, but there is something that will always be: love.

Today's Date:

This quote inspires the following thoughts in me:

This quote inspires me to take these actions today:

(Before bedtime) I accomplished these actions today:

"There has to be evil so that good can prove its purity above it." - The Buddha

It is an undeniable truth that evil is present in the world. The task of every human being on earth is to do good deeds, act righteously, and oppose evil in order to defeat it. Evil cannot win in the face of overwhelming love.

Today's Date:

This quote inspires the following thoughts in me:

This quote inspires me to take these actions today:

(Before bedtime) I accomplished these actions today:

"Not everyone will understand your journey. That's okay. You're here to live your life not to make everyone understand." - The Buddha

There are many times in life that others will question our choices. Sometimes the reasoning behind a decision is not understood or it can be a difference of opinion. To some, this may seem like a difficult hurdle to overcome, but the most important thing is to live your own life. It is impossible to please everyone and there is no need for you to try.

Today's Date:

This quote inspires the following thoughts in me:

This quote inspires me to take these actions today:

(Before bedtime) I accomplished these actions today:

"Meditation brings wisdom; lack of meditation leaves ignorance. Know well what leads you forward and what holds you back, and choose the path that leads to wisdom."- The Buddha

Every day we have a choice to wake up and choose whether or not we will be guided by the fog of the past or the clarity of the present. The more we know how to connect to our own inner wisdom, the easier it becomes to see what's really going on in this very moment. Meditation helps you to see your path clearly.

Today's Date:

This quote inspires the following thoughts in me:

This quote inspires me to take these actions today:

(Before bedtime) I accomplished these actions today:

"The mind contains all possibilities."
- The Buddha

We often don't realize how much of an impact our thoughts can have. Our thoughts become words, and these words create the reality we live in. Thoughts don't happen in isolation either; they happen on a continuum of possibility that begins with the quantum field and extends to every point in our lives. This is because what we think, we create.

Today's Date:

This quote inspires the following thoughts in me:

This quote inspires me to take these actions today:

(Before bedtime) I accomplished these actions today:

"Forget who hurt you yesterday, but don't forget those who love you every day." - The Buddha

Some people may be hurtful and cruel to others, but there are also those who show love and kindness. These individuals should be a priority for you in your life. Focusing on those that hurt people will only bring you more pain and misery. How can we change the world if we choose to focus on those who don't practice kindness?

Today's Date:

This quote inspires the following thoughts in me:

This quote inspires me to take these actions today:

(Before bedtime) I accomplished these actions today:

"Understand that you own nothing; everything that surrounds you is temporary, only the love in your heart will last forever." - The Buddha

In life, we often find ourselves so consumed by the materialistic things around us that we forget to enjoy what matters most. Although it may be hard to think about, everything that surrounds us is temporary. Just believe that the love in your heart will last forever when everything around you dissolves into dust.

Today's Date:

This quote inspires the following thoughts in me:

This quote inspires me to take these actions today:

(Before bedtime) I accomplished these actions today:

"Have compassion for all beings, rich and poor alike; each has their suffering. Some suffer too much, others too little." - The Buddha

We live in a world with many disparities. It is important to try and be compassionate to all beings, rich and poor alike. We should not lose sight of the fact that every person has their own unique suffering. Even though we can't fix all of these inequities, we can relieve the burden of all those we come into contact with acts of kindness and compassion.

Today's Date:

This quote inspires the following thoughts in me:

This quote inspires me to take these actions today:

(Before bedtime) I accomplished these actions today:

"The man who foolishly does me wrong, I will return to him the protection of my most ungrudging love; and the more evil comes from him, the more good shall go from me." - The Buddha

The only way to conquer the animus of someone who would hurt you is to respond with kindness and compassion. Kindness and compassion will overpower their attempt at harm. Even a simple smile can disarm a person's anger.

Today's Date:

This quote inspires the following thoughts in me:

This quote inspires me to take these actions today:

(Before bedtime) I accomplished these actions today:

"Don't think too much. Just do what makes you happy."
- The Buddha

When people think too much about something, it often causes them to make a decision not to do anything at all, which means that they won't be happy with any outcome. Do you allow yourself to do the things that make you happy?

Today's Date:

This quote inspires the following thoughts in me:

This quote inspires me to take these actions today:

(Before bedtime) I accomplished these actions today:

"When you move your focus from competition to contribution life becomes a celebration."
- The Buddha

In a world where people are constantly competing with one another, it can be difficult to shift from focusing on being better than others to being better for the world. In your everyday life, shift your focus to acts of kindness and compassion, and you'll quickly see the joy you bring into the world.

Today's Date:

This quote inspires the following thoughts in me:

This quote inspires me to take these actions today:

(Before bedtime) I accomplished these actions today:

"Forgive people in your life, even those who are not sorry for their actions. Holding on to anger only hurts you not them." - The Buddha

It is hard to let go of the anger, disappointment, and sadness we feel when someone has hurt us. But holding on to those feelings hurts us long after the person who wronged us has forgotten about the pain he caused. You can make the decision to let it go. Show yourself the kindness and compassion that you deserve.

Today's Date:

This quote inspires the following thoughts in me:

This quote inspires me to take these actions today:

(Before bedtime) I accomplished these actions today:

"Think good thoughts say nice things, do good for others. Everything comes back." - The Buddha

Just like the universe, karma is a complicated concept. Some people believe that everything happens for a reason, good or bad. Others believe that if you do something with good intentions, it will come back to you tenfold. Which is the better way to live? Have you experienced karma in your life?

Today's Date:

This quote inspires the following thoughts in me:

This quote inspires me to take these actions today:

(Before bedtime) I accomplished these actions today:

"Many do not realize that we here must die. For those who realize this, quarrels end." - The Buddha

Do you ever get tired of the fighting? All the arguments, all the misunderstandings? It's time to put an end to it. Life is too short to spend your time in anger and fighting. But life is just long enough to share the love in your heart widely. Will you?

Today's Date:

This quote inspires the following thoughts in me:

This quote inspires me to take these actions today:

(Before bedtime) I accomplished these actions today:

"When you stop trying to change others and work on yourself, your world changes for the better."
- The Buddha

The idea that we can somehow change another person is a fallacy. When we stop trying to "fix" the people in our lives and instead focus our attention on becoming kinder and more compassionate ourselves, we begin to see our world for what it really is. Only then are we able to create a happier world for ourselves and those who surround us.

Today's Date:

This quote inspires the following thoughts in me:

This quote inspires me to take these actions today:

(Before bedtime) I accomplished these actions today:

"Do not give up your authority and follow blindly the will of others. This way will lead to only delusion."
- The Buddha

Do not follow anyone else's direction without first asking if it is true to what you know. You must only follow what you know to be true in your heart. Following this rule will give you control of your mind and your world.

Today's Date:

This quote inspires the following thoughts in me:

This quote inspires me to take these actions today:

(Before bedtime) I accomplished these actions today:

"Master your words. Master your thoughts. Never allow your body to do harm. Follow these three roads with purity and you will find yourself upon the one way, the way of wisdom." - The Buddha

In order to become wise, we must first master ourselves- our words, actions, and deeds. By being kind we can see the world from other people's perspectives and understand their feelings. Through thinking deeply we get a better understanding of the world around us and the people who inhabit it. And by performing good deeds can we make a direct impact on others.

Today's Date:

This quote inspires the following thoughts in me:

This quote inspires me to take these actions today:

(Before bedtime) I accomplished these actions today:

"As an elephant in the battlefield withstands arrows shot from bows all around, even so shall I endure abuse." - The Buddha

It is easy to become angry when someone is trying to hurt you. When this happens, it can be difficult to stand strong and endure the pain without retaliating. Take their abuse without becoming angry or abusive in return - you will always win the battle.

Today's Date:

This quote inspires the following thoughts in me:

This quote inspires me to take these actions today:

(Before bedtime) I accomplished these actions today:

"Never fear what will become of you, depend on no one. Only the moment you reject all help are you freed." - The Buddha

When you reach the point in your life that you believe in your own ability, and know that you can face any challenge on your own, you become completely free. Self-reliance is truly liberating. The person with this knowledge knows they are not completely dependent on others to get through the challenges of their life.

Today's Date:

This quote inspires the following thoughts in me:

This quote inspires me to take these actions today:

(Before bedtime) I accomplished these actions today:

"Always be mindful of the kindness and not the faults of others." - The Buddha

One of the most important things one can do to make the world a better place is to be mindful of others' kindness and ignore their faults. When we are kind to someone even though they hurt us, offend us, or might not deserve it, it encourages them to be kinder and kinder.

Today's Date:

This quote inspires the following thoughts in me:

This quote inspires me to take these actions today:

(Before bedtime) I accomplished these actions today:

"Want what you have and you will always get what you want." - The Buddha

We are constantly surrounded by people who have more. The culture of consumerism says that if you don't have it, you will be unhappy and unfulfilled. But this is not the case. There is a difference between being content and happy with what you have, and suffering because you don't have something. There is peace in being content with where you are now, and what you have now.

Today's Date:

This quote inspires the following thoughts in me:

This quote inspires me to take these actions today:

(Before bedtime) I accomplished these actions today:

"He who does not understand your silence will probably not understand your words." - The Buddha

Sometimes the wisest people say very little, waiting for the appropriate time to say only what is most important and most helpful to the conversation. They often listen well and thoughtfully, not judging or interrupting. Reflect for a moment: Do you wait for the right moment to say what needs to be said?

Today's Date:

This quote inspires the following thoughts in me:

This quote inspires me to take these actions today:

(Before bedtime) I accomplished these actions today:

"If you find someone with wisdom, good judgment,
and good actions; make him a companion."
- The Buddha

If you recognize wisdom, good judgement, and good actions in someone else, then they are a good person and someone worth keeping as a friend. They will bring out the best in you and help you grow. Who in your life comes to mind?

Today's Date:

This quote inspires the following thoughts in me:

This quote inspires me to take these actions today:

(Before bedtime) I accomplished these actions today:

"Three things cannot be long hidden: the sun, the moon, and the truth." - The Buddha

It is easy to see why so many people distrust each other nowadays. Lies and deceit are everywhere, and it often seems like the only thing that will never change. However, there is always hope in knowing that truth will prevail in the end. When you recognize loving-kindness in others, in their words, in their deeds, you will have found truth.

Today's Date:

This quote inspires the following thoughts in me:

This quote inspires me to take these actions today:

(Before bedtime) I accomplished these actions today:

"No one saves us but ourselves. No one can and no one may. We ourselves must walk the path."
- The Buddha

When we accept full responsibility for our own happiness, we are free of outside sources that may provide us with temporary gratification, but ultimately leave us feeling empty. Furthermore, when we rely on ourselves, we gain the confidence and strength to face any challenge that comes along on our journey towards living an authentic life.

Today's Date:

This quote inspires the following thoughts in me:

This quote inspires me to take these actions today:

(Before bedtime) I accomplished these actions today:

"Ceasing to do evil, cultivating the good, purifying the heart: this is the teaching of the Buddhas."
- The Buddha

Is there really anything more important to living a good life than doing no evil, cultivating good actions, and staying pure of heart? But how do accomplish this day after day? How will you demonstrate the purity of your heart today?

Today's Date:

This quote inspires the following thoughts in me:

This quote inspires me to take these actions today:

(Before bedtime) I accomplished these actions today:

"Virtue is persecuted more by the wicked than it is loved by the good." - The Buddha

The wicked person attacks virtue in others, while the virtuous person recognizes the good in the wicked. Why does the wicked person get more attention?

Today's Date:

This quote inspires the following thoughts in me:

This quote inspires me to take these actions today:

(Before bedtime) I accomplished these actions today:

"In whom there is no sympathy for living beings: know him as an outcast." - The Buddha

It is always unfortunate when you encounter someone who has no empathy for other human beings. Someone who cannot feel compassion or kindness for others is likely to do anything they can to help themselves, regardless of any harm to others. When you see someone without empathy, avoid him at all costs and he will not be able to add any negativity to your world.

Today's Date:

This quote inspires the following thoughts in me:

This quote inspires me to take these actions today:

(Before bedtime) I accomplished these actions today:

"The external world is only a manifestation of the activities of the mind itself, and the mind grasps it as an external world simply because of its habit of discrimination and false-reasoning. Look at things truthfully." - The Buddha

We often fool ourselves into thinking that the external world is not connected with us. Understand that you create your world. For example, if you are feeling happy one day, then your environment may appear to be more vibrant. Conversely, if you are feeling sad one day, then your environment may appear to be darker. You are more powerful than you realize.

Today's Date:

This quote inspires the following thoughts in me:

This quote inspires me to take these actions today:

(Before bedtime) I accomplished these actions today:

"I never see what has been done; I only see what remains to be done." - The Buddha

Most of us think about our past accomplishments. We reminisce about the things we have done and wonder, "Was I good enough?" Meanwhile, we forget about what good is left to do. The realization that there are so many more opportunities than just those that already occurred can be inspiring. It's not about how happy you are with what you have accomplished; it's all about what good you can do next.

Today's Date:

This quote inspires the following thoughts in me:

This quote inspires me to take these actions today:

(Before bedtime) I accomplished these actions today:

"Those who have failed to work toward the truth have missed the purpose of living." - The Buddha

The purpose of living is to explore the meaning of life and make a difference in the world. Those who have failed to work toward this truth have missed out on the opportunity to live a fulfilling life. In order to make a difference, one has to explore all aspects of life and not stop until they find what is right for them.

Today's Date:

This quote inspires the following thoughts in me:

This quote inspires me to take these actions today:

(Before bedtime) I accomplished these actions today:

"Better than a thousand hollow words is one word that brings peace." - The Buddha

In a world where words can be taken as a joke, a weapon, or just a way to keep the conversation going, finding one word that is meaningful and has a positive impact on all those hearing it can be difficult. Seek out moments each day to bring peace and compassion to those you converse with.

Today's Date:

This quote inspires the following thoughts in me:

This quote inspires me to take these actions today:

(Before bedtime) I accomplished these actions today:

"Trust yourself, you've survived a lot and you'll survive what's coming." - The Buddha

It is sometimes hard to imagine that we will ever be able to get through what's coming next. The one thing we can do is learn to trust ourselves. We have come this far on our own and we will be able to get through and what life brings to us on our own as well.

Today's Date:

This quote inspires the following thoughts in me:

This quote inspires me to take these actions today:

(Before bedtime) I accomplished these actions today:

"Man's troubles are rooted in extreme attention to senses, thoughts, and imagination. Attention should be focused internally to experience a quiet body and a calm mind." - The Buddha

Living in a world dominated by the senses can be trying. Our thoughts and imagination can run rampant, preventing us from focusing on what is happening in the present moment. The way to escape the crowded mind is to turn inward and focus on what is happening internally. A quiet body and calm mind will allow one to experience greater peace than they ever thought possible.

Today's Date:

This quote inspires the following thoughts in me:

This quote inspires me to take these actions today:

(Before bedtime) I accomplished these actions today:

"If you let cloudy water settle, it will become clear. If you let your upset mind settle, your course will also become clear." - The Buddha

When we give ourselves time to calm down and take a break from any difficult situation, we can see the situation more clearly and choose which course of action we want to take next. We can learn to clear our minds through the practice of meditation, which serves to prepare us for "cloudy waters."

Today's Date:

This quote inspires the following thoughts in me:

This quote inspires me to take these actions today:

(Before bedtime) I accomplished these actions today:

"Love the whole world as a mother loves her only child." - The Buddha

Direct all your love and kindness to the world to give peace and comfort to those who need it most. When just one other person extends that same kindness and compassion out to others, then it brings peace and comfort to not only those people who need it most but also everyone around them.

Today's Date:

This quote inspires the following thoughts in me:

This quote inspires me to take these actions today:

(Before bedtime) I accomplished these actions today:

"The mind is not a dustbin to keep anger, hatred and jealousy. But it is the treasure box to keep, love happiness and sweet memories." - The Buddha

If there is one secret to a happy life, it may be the ability to release the negative emotions that prevent us from opening our heart to others. When we let go of the negativity in our lives and open up to others with love and compassion, we experience true happiness. The secret to living a happy life is taking every opportunity to share positive feelings with others.

Today's Date:

This quote inspires the following thoughts in me:

This quote inspires me to take these actions today:

(Before bedtime) I accomplished these actions today:

"Do not judge yourself harshly. Without mercy for ourselves, we cannot love the world."
- The Buddha

Have you ever been told to "quit being so hard on yourself?" It may seem like a simple phrase, but it actually means quite a lot. In order for us to love the world, we must love ourselves first. Without mercy for ourselves, we cannot show mercy to others. How deeply do you love yourself?

Today's Date:

This quote inspires the following thoughts in me:

This quote inspires me to take these actions today:

(Before bedtime) I accomplished these actions today:

"All human unhappiness comes from not facing reality squarely, exactly as it is." - The Buddha

We all know that it can be hard to face reality, especially if it is not what we want it to be. We may feel ashamed of our past choices or unfulfilled by the present moment. However, seeing reality for what it is does help us cope with life better and will make us happier and more compassionate people in the end.

Today's Date:

This quote inspires the following thoughts in me:

This quote inspires me to take these actions today:

(Before bedtime) I accomplished these actions today:

"Generosity brings happiness at every stage of its expression. We experience joy in forming the intention to be generous. We experience joy in the actual act of giving something. And we experience joy in remembering the fact that we have given."
- The Buddha

Generosity is an expression of love which has the power to bring happiness at every stage. How do we approach each day with a plan to be generous? Through kind words, random acts of kindness, a smile at someone who looks down? Consciously plan to be generous with your kindness today.

Today's Date:

This quote inspires the following thoughts in me:

This quote inspires me to take these actions today:

(Before bedtime) I accomplished these actions today:

"Freedom and happiness are found in the flexibility and ease with which we move through change."
- The Buddha

People often find it hard to change, but the struggle isn't necessary. It is possible to make changes in our lives that can bring us joy and happiness. Let go of what is no longer serving you and embrace the new and exciting things that come with change. The more you embrace changes, the more content you'll be in your life.

Today's Date:

This quote inspires the following thoughts in me:

This quote inspires me to take these actions today:

(Before bedtime) I accomplished these actions today:

"Karma grows from our hearts. Karma terminates from our hearts. Karma has no menu. You get served what you deserve." - The Buddha

Karma is the principle that our actions and intent in this life will determine our karma in the future. Karma can be seen as positive or negative depending on someone's intentions. So it's important to think about what you do and why you do it before it comes back to you. Listen to your heart, and do the right thing always.

Today's Date:

This quote inspires the following thoughts in me:

This quote inspires me to take these actions today:

(Before bedtime) I accomplished these actions today:

"Each day of your life you are sowing seeds that one day you will harvest." - The Buddha

As you go about your day, remember that each action you take will either be a seed for the future or a weed that will choke out any new growth. For some, each day of your life can feel like it is just one more day of monotony and boredom. But, if you just take time to look around, there are seeds being planted on any given day. No matter what you do, what you say, or where you go- there are seeds being planted. Today, will you plant weeds or flowers?

Today's Date:

This quote inspires the following thoughts in me:

This quote inspires me to take these actions today:

(Before bedtime) I accomplished these actions today:

"You need to love yourself. Love yourself so much to the point that your energy and aura rejects anyone who doesn't know your worth." - The Buddha

Loving yourself is not an easy task. It's a daily struggle against the voices in your head telling you that you are not good enough, and it's a battle to overcome any past hurt or trauma that might still be lingering in the back of your mind. Loving yourself is not about being self-centered or conceited. It's about accepting your flaws and finding the good in you, and ignoring the people who would bring you down.

Today's Date:

This quote inspires the following thoughts in me:

This quote inspires me to take these actions today:

(Before bedtime) I accomplished these actions today:

"Treat others with respect. How you treat others will be how they treat you." - The Buddha

The author Stephen Covey said: "Treat people as if they were what they ought to be and you help them become what they are capable of being. Do you know someone that treats you poorly, or is always rude to you? How can you help them grow into the best person they can be?

Today's Date:

This quote inspires the following thoughts in me:

This quote inspires me to take these actions today:

(Before bedtime) I accomplished these actions today:

"Most problems, if you give them enough time and space, will eventually wear themselves out."
- The Buddha

Sometimes we rush to solve a problem without really understanding it or how it affects us, and find that the problem doesn't really exist. In fact, the solution is often the opportunity for a little break from stress. Take time to work through your problem before making any rash decisions. The problem may dissolve on its own like fog in the late morning.

Today's Date:

This quote inspires the following thoughts in me:

This quote inspires me to take these actions today:

(Before bedtime) I accomplished these actions today:

"Our theories of the eternal are as valuable as are those which a chick which has not broken its way through its shell might form of the outside world." - The Buddha

We should be more humble when it comes to professing knowledge about the eternal. Each day we may peck away at the shell, but like the chick in the egg, we're hardly out of it yet. Instead, we should focus on what we are experiencing in this moment. This moment provides an opportunity to see the truth of our existence. Let's focus on that.

Today's Date:

This quote inspires the following thoughts in me:

This quote inspires me to take these actions today:

(Before bedtime) I accomplished these actions today:

"To find peace, sometimes you have to be willing to lose your connection with people, places, and things that create all the noise in your life." - The Buddha

Whether it's the spinning of your mind, the buzzing sound from your phone, or constant negative thoughts that keep you from being fully present in any given moment, you are constantly surrounded by noise. That's why at times you have to be willing to say goodbye to people, places, and things that create all the noise in your life - and find instead, quiet and peace.

Today's Date:

This quote inspires the following thoughts in me:

This quote inspires me to take these actions today:

(Before bedtime) I accomplished these actions today:

"Don't allow someone to treat you poorly just because you love them." - The Buddha

When you love someone, you're willing to forgive them for their mistakes. It becomes so easy to overlook the other person's faults because you love them so much. But a line is crossed when the person you love treats you poorly, and you must not allow it to continue. Every person deserves to be treated with respect. You should not settle for anything less than respect from the person who you love the most.

Today's Date:

This quote inspires the following thoughts in me:

This quote inspires me to take these actions today:

(Before bedtime) I accomplished these actions today:

"Better it is to speak an unpleasant truth than to tell lies." - The Buddha

In our society, we have become desensitized to truth and honesty. In our day-to-day lives, people commonly lie for their own benefit or that of another person. A lack of self-awareness and empathy often leaves us justifying our lies as necessary falsehoods. This kind of thinking only reinforces a false reality where dishonesty becomes more desirable than honesty. When is a "white" lie acceptable? When is it better to tell the truth?

Today's Date:

This quote inspires the following thoughts in me:

This quote inspires me to take these actions today:

(Before bedtime) I accomplished these actions today:

"The secret of health for both mind and body is not to mourn for the past, not to worry about the future, not to anticipate the future, but to live the present moment wisely and earnestly." - The Buddha

Mindfulness can be defined as the act of being aware of one's thoughts, feelings, bodily sensations, surroundings, and environment in this moment. It's so easy to get caught up in what is coming next or what you wish was happening now. Living in the present gives you a chance to be mindful of what really matters to you at this particular time and enjoy it for all its worth before it passes away too.

Today's Date:

This quote inspires the following thoughts in me:

This quote inspires me to take these actions today:

(Before bedtime) I accomplished these actions today:

"There is nothing so disobedient as an undisciplined mind, and there is nothing so obedient as a disciplined mind." - The Buddha

What can help you achieve success in life? What are the important steps to take, that will lead to a meaningful and rewarding career? If you have an undisciplined mind, chances are you have failed at many things in your life; and if you have a disciplined mind, then you've succeeded. Discipline is the one thing that will get you to the desired end result: happiness and success.

Today's Date:

This quote inspires the following thoughts in me:

This quote inspires me to take these actions today:

(Before bedtime) I accomplished these actions today:

"Long is the night to him who is awake; long is a mile to him who is tired; long is life to the foolish who do not know the true law." - The Buddha

No matter how bad things seem to be, it is much better to live in this moment. Many people are quick to forget the good moments of the past, but regret it later when they are too busy trying to prepare for the future. It's important to enjoy what you have now while you can because who knows what may happen tomorrow.

Today's Date:

This quote inspires the following thoughts in me:

This quote inspires me to take these actions today:

(Before bedtime) I accomplished these actions today:

"Hatred does not cease through hatred at any time. Hatred ceases through love." - The Buddha

How to end the cycle of violence and hatred that plagues society today? We may embody kindness in our gentle yet firm approach to life, creating a peaceful revolution where people were able to live in harmony without anger or resentment.

Today's Date:

This quote inspires the following thoughts in me:

This quote inspires me to take these actions today:

(Before bedtime) I accomplished these actions today:

"What we are today comes from our thoughts of yesterday, and our present thoughts build our life of tomorrow: Our life is the creation of our mind."
- The Buddha

While most people believe they are not in control of their lives, they are actually at the mercy of past thoughts - past thoughts that have come to fruition. What we think about in this current moment is what shapes our future. That means that this moment, and how you use this moment, shapes your entire future.

Today's Date:

This quote inspires the following thoughts in me:

This quote inspires me to take these actions today:

(Before bedtime) I accomplished these actions today:

"Meditation brings wisdom; lack of meditation leaves ignorance. Know well what leads you forward and what hold you back, and choose the path that leads to wisdom." The Buddha

Meditation is a practice that has benefits for one's physical, mental and emotional health. However, the most important benefit of meditation is that it can help bring wisdom to a person's life. Meditation can lead to greater self-awareness and an increased understanding about oneself. Doesn't it make sense to take a few moments out of each day to quietly look within?

Today's Date:

This quote inspires the following thoughts in me:

This quote inspires me to take these actions today:

(Before bedtime) I accomplished these actions today:

"Avoid evil deeds as a man who loves life avoids poison." - The Buddha

We cannot truly understand the meaning of our existence if we don't take time to contemplate and evaluate what we put into this world. All we ask of ourselves is to live a life filled with good deeds - for our own sake and the sake of those around us. Living a life filled with good deeds brings us closer to discovering the truth of our existence, and closer to achieving the happiness we all seek from our life.

Today's Date:

This quote inspires the following thoughts in me:

This quote inspires me to take these actions today:

(Before bedtime) I accomplished these actions today:

"If the problem can be solved why worry? If the problem cannot be solved worrying will do you no good." - The Buddha

Do you find that you worry about things more than you need to? If so, let your worrying go. Worrying doesn't help with solving the problem at hand. In fact it may cloud your mind with negativity which can make it harder to think clearly. So relax. Take some deep breaths and just relax. This problem will pass.

Today's Date:

This quote inspires the following thoughts in me:

This quote inspires me to take these actions today:

(Before bedtime) I accomplished these actions today:

"He who experiences the unity of life sees his own Self in all beings, and all beings in his own Self, and looks on everything with an impartial eye." - The Buddha

The harm done in this world is often rooted in the inability to see the unity of all life, and to recognize our own self in all beings and vice versa. This is a philosophy that respects and reveres all living things and sees them as interconnected and interdependent. It's a way of looking at the world that promotes impartiality and compassion for others.

Today's Date:

This quote inspires the following thoughts in me:

This quote inspires me to take these actions today:

(Before bedtime) I accomplished these actions today:

"If you are quiet enough, you will hear the flow of the universe. You will feel its rhythm. Go with this flow. Happiness lies ahead." - The Buddha

If you are true and quiet and still enough, and allow everything to happen as it will without trying to control the outcome of every event, you will find happiness. There is a natural rhythm to life. Go with it and you will find happiness for all eternity.

Today's Date:

This quote inspires the following thoughts in me:

This quote inspires me to take these actions today:

(Before bedtime) I accomplished these actions today:

"As irrigators lead water where they want, as archers make their arrows straight, as carpenters carve wood, the wise shape their minds." - The Buddha

A mind is like a muscle; it can be strengthened with use, and it can grow weaker with neglect. First begin by looking at your own thoughts and actions and honestly assessing them. It is only then that you can start working on strengthening your mind and seeing the truth in all things while also becoming wiser.

Today's Date:

This quote inspires the following thoughts in me:

This quote inspires me to take these actions today:

(Before bedtime) I accomplished these actions today:

"Darkness cannot drive out darkness; only light can do that. Hate cannot drive out hate; only love can do that." - The Buddha

We are living in an era where hatred is on the rise. All around us, we see people scapegoated for the problems of society, and on social media, we see rampant hate speech. It seems like it's easy to point to one group or another as our cause of all the world's wrongs. But what if this isn't true? What if love is the answer instead?

Today's Date:

This quote inspires the following thoughts in me:

This quote inspires me to take these actions today:

(Before bedtime) I accomplished these actions today:

"The best love is the one that makes you a better person, without changing you into someone other than yourself." - The Buddha

The best love is the kind that allows you to be your true self without fear of judgment or ridicule. It's the type of love that encourages you to make mistakes and learn from them. It provides the kind of stability and confidence necessary for living authentically, happily, and confidently.

Today's Date:

This quote inspires the following thoughts in me:

This quote inspires me to take these actions today:

(Before bedtime) I accomplished these actions today:

"Speak only endearing speech, speech that is welcomed. Speech, when it brings no evil to others, is a pleasant thing." - The Buddha

We all know how much we enjoy other people's company when they speak only nice things about life and never bring up any subjects that cause other people pain. Wouldn't it be nice if everyone followed this advice? Do you?

Today's Date:

This quote inspires the following thoughts in me:

This quote inspires me to take these actions today:

(Before bedtime) I accomplished these actions today:

"Dignity and quiet joy in all that we do are the expressions of perfect concentration and perfect wisdom." - The Buddha

There are two ways to live one's life, with dignity and quiet joy in all that we do or with fear, uncertainty, and deep regret. To live a life of dignity and joy there needs to be perfect concentration and wisdom. Perfect concentration is the ability to dwell cheerfully on the present moment without being distracted. Perfect wisdom is understanding how everything changes- how nothing lasts forever or remains unchanged. With these two skills, it becomes easier for us to accept what comes our way.

Today's Date:

This quote inspires the following thoughts in me:

This quote inspires me to take these actions today:

(Before bedtime) I accomplished these actions today:

"Praise and blame, gain and loss, pleasure and sorrow come and go like the wind. To be happy, rest like a giant tree in the midst of them all." - The Buddha

There is no one who does not experience stress and worry in their life. We all have adversity, but it's how we deal with those obstacles that will either make us stronger or leave us with regrets. Some people find it easy to not dwell on things they can't change, but for others it can be difficult to avoid the worries of the world. How will you react to the challenges you face today?

Today's Date:

This quote inspires the following thoughts in me:

This quote inspires me to take these actions today:

(Before bedtime) I accomplished these actions today:

"To be selfish, greedy, and unwilling to help the needy gives rise to future starvation and clothlessness."
- The Buddha

People who are unselfish and willing to help those in need will give rise to a better society and a happier life for themselves as well as the people around them. It's much easier to be generous and selfless than greedy and selfish, and it leads you and the rest of the world to a better place.

Today's Date:

This quote inspires the following thoughts in me:

This quote inspires me to take these actions today:

(Before bedtime) I accomplished these actions today:

"Good health is simply the slowest way a human being can die." - The Buddha

The activities we do in our daily lives, such as eating, exercising, and sleeping, are the best things to do for our bodies. Taking care of our body is just as important as taking care of our mind. Our mental health can be impacted by the way we take care of ourselves physically, and will affect how happy and compassionate we are day to day.

Today's Date:

This quote inspires the following thoughts in me:

This quote inspires me to take these actions today:

(Before bedtime) I accomplished these actions today:

"Pain is inevitable; suffering is optional." - The Buddha

Emotional pain is inevitable in life, but suffering is actually a choice. Life can be a roller coaster of ups and downs with emotions ranging from happiness to sadness. Although it's unavoidable, the degree of emotional pain you experience can be managed through self-acceptance and self-compassion. Are you in control of your mind? Are you abundantly self-compassionate?

Today's Date:

This quote inspires the following thoughts in me:

This quote inspires me to take these actions today:

(Before bedtime) I accomplished these actions today:

"Friendship is the only cure for hatred, the only guarantee of peace." - The Buddha

When we feel the pain caused by the actions of others, with all its ugliness and injustice, it can be easy to give in and surrender to hate. But history teaches us that it is only with kindness, understanding and acceptance that we can avoid the follies of hatred. With these three simple virtues, we can transform enemies into friends, and leave hatred behind.

Today's Date:

This quote inspires the following thoughts in me:

This quote inspires me to take these actions today:

(Before bedtime) I accomplished these actions today:

"There is nothing more dreadful than the habit of doubt. Doubt separates people. It is a poison that disintegrates friendships and breaks up pleasant relations. It is a thorn that irritates and hurts; it is a sword that kills." - The Buddha

Doubt is a dark and poisonous force that destroys the happiness of all who let it in. It is an evil beast that consumes your life, crippling you with uncertainty and pessimism. But the light of truth has a way to expel doubt from its lair. How will you seek out the truth?

Today's Date:

This quote inspires the following thoughts in me:

This quote inspires me to take these actions today:

(Before bedtime) I accomplished these actions today:

"Every experience, no matter how bad it seems, holds within a blessing of some kind. The goal is to find it."
- The Buddha

In order to find a blessing in any experience, it is important to make observation of what has been given. In each moment, the seeker of the blessing must allow for change and growth without resistance. One cannot find anything they are not looking for. Anything we need we already have because we are one with everything and everyone. Look within.

Today's Date:

This quote inspires the following thoughts in me:

This quote inspires me to take these actions today:

(Before bedtime) I accomplished these actions today:

"Many people will walk in and out of your life. But only true friends will leave footprints in your heart."
- The Buddha

You may find that there are some people who will be at the same places you are for a fleeting moment, then disappear into the abyss. They never had any intention of staying, yet their presence was felt. There are also those that seem to be on a continuous loop, always coming back to you no matter how much they stray away. What kind of friend do you want? What kind of friend are you?

Today's Date:

This quote inspires the following thoughts in me:

This quote inspires me to take these actions today:

(Before bedtime) I accomplished these actions today:

"To keep the body in good health is a duty, otherwise we shall not be able to keep our mind strong and clear." - The Buddha

Being healthy and exercising your body goes hand in hand with being healthy and exercising your mind. When you take care of your body, you're treating yourself to a life full of health and happiness. Similarly, when you challenge your mind to see the truth, it's an opportunity for growth and improvement. The more we exercise both our minds and bodies the better we feel, and the more we are able to interact with the world with loving kindness.

Today's Date:

This quote inspires the following thoughts in me:

This quote inspires me to take these actions today:

(Before bedtime) I accomplished these actions today:

"Drop by drop is the water pot filled. Likewise, the wise man, gathering it little by little, fills himself with good." - The Buddha

Wisdom is not gained all at once. It is slowly accumulated over our lifetime, if we allow it to fill our being. Each day is an opportunity to learn more. Are you open to gaining wisdom every day? How will you fill your pot with wisdom today?

Today's Date:

This quote inspires the following thoughts in me:

This quote inspires me to take these actions today:

(Before bedtime) I accomplished these actions today:

"However many holy words you read, however many you speak, what good will they do you if you do not act on upon them?" - The Buddha

Our actions are what make us who we are. What you say or think doesn't matter if it doesn't lead to any change in how you behave. In the end, your actions are what will be judged. Will you look for opportunities - small and large - to do good today?

Today's Date:

This quote inspires the following thoughts in me:

This quote inspires me to take these actions today:

(Before bedtime) I accomplished these actions today:

"Let us rise up and be thankful, for if we didn't learn a lot today, at least we learned a little, and if we didn't learn a little, at least we didn't get sick, and if we got sick, at least we didn't die; so, let us all be thankful."
- The Buddha

Be thankful at the end of every day for the blessings, small and large, that came your way. Take a moment to reflect on all the good things you have about you. It's empowering to see what you have accomplished and it will help you grow in character and wisdom each day.

Today's Date:

This quote inspires the following thoughts in me:

This quote inspires me to take these actions today:

(Before bedtime) I accomplished these actions today:

"He who sits alone, sleeps alone, and walks alone, who is strenuous and subdues himself alone, will find delight in the solitude of the forest." - The Buddha

Solitude offers an opportunity to explore oneself without judgment. It's a time for introspection, reflection, and mindfulness - a chance to be creative or simply take a break from the overwhelm of the world. The best part of solitude is the total lack of distraction. No one wants to hear about your day when you are alone. There are no interruptions or potential distractions, just you and your thoughts. In daily meditation you will find peace that lasts.

Today's Date:

This quote inspires the following thoughts in me:

This quote inspires me to take these actions today:

(Before bedtime) I accomplished these actions today:

"To understand everything is to forgive everything."
- The Buddha

When we understand the interconnectedness of everyone and everything in this world, it is easier to forgive those who have hurt us. By forgiving someone else for the wrongs they have done we are sharing our compassion with the entire world, making everyone's existence a little bit better.

Today's Date:

This quote inspires the following thoughts in me:

This quote inspires me to take these actions today:

(Before bedtime) I accomplished these actions today:

"Life is like a book. Some chapters sad, some happy and some exciting. But if you never turn the page you will never know what the next chapter holds."
- The Buddha

You never know what is going to happen in your life. There will be moments where you feel like you're not sure which way to turn, but just keep going. Remember that there is always something that will bring you back to happiness and joy. You just have to find the path that takes you there.

Today's Date:

This quote inspires the following thoughts in me:

This quote inspires me to take these actions today:

(Before bedtime) I accomplished these actions today:

"If you truly loved yourself, you could never hurt another." - The Buddha

It's difficult to understand why people consciously choose to hurt others, because the world is one interconnected entity. All beings are made up of the same stuff - matter and energy. When we have complete love and compassion for ourselves, we can't possible wish anything less for others in this world.

Today's Date:

This quote inspires the following thoughts in me:

This quote inspires me to take these actions today:

(Before bedtime) I accomplished these actions today:

"Life is so very difficult. How can we be anything but kind?" - The Buddha

Everyone has their fair share of pain in life. No one gets through life without some form of difficulties, so it is important to be kind to everyone you meet because who knows what they are going through. Even if no one has hurt them, they could have faced other obstacles in their life which are just as tough. If we all try to be more compassionate and kind, we can make this world a better place.

Today's Date:

This quote inspires the following thoughts in me:

This quote inspires me to take these actions today:

(Before bedtime) I accomplished these actions today:

"Happiness does not depend on what you have or who you are. It solely relies on what you think."
- The Buddha

Even if you are born into the richest family in the world, happiness is not guaranteed. Happiness is not something that you can buy or find anywhere external of yourself. Happiness only exists when you search for it within. You create it yourself through your thoughts and actions.

Today's Date:

This quote inspires the following thoughts in me:

This quote inspires me to take these actions today:

(Before bedtime) I accomplished these actions today:

"How people treat you is their karma; how you react is yours." - The Buddha

It's never easy to forgive someone for hurting us, but in order to move on with our lives, we need to let go of the negative feelings associated with the situation. But more than this, forgive yourself for allowing them to hurt you. The wounds inflicted by others will not heal until we realize that they can only hurt us if we give them permission to.

Today's Date:

This quote inspires the following thoughts in me:

This quote inspires me to take these actions today:

(Before bedtime) I accomplished these actions today:

"Everything that has a beginning has an ending."
- The Buddha

No matter how hard we try to hold on, all things eventually come to an end. With the passage of time, our surroundings change. People come and go, relationships grow and fade, commitments are fulfilled, and careers are realized. There is no escaping this universal truth. The wonderful news is that when we live fully in this moment, we are experiencing the best of life as it unfolds.

Today's Date:

This quote inspires the following thoughts in me:

This quote inspires me to take these actions today:

(Before bedtime) I accomplished these actions today:

"Mind precedes all mental states. Mind is their chief; they are all mind-wrought." - The Buddha

One who looks closely sees that an evil or unwholesome event has its roots in the mind, sees that the mind is stained by the colors of greed, aversion, and delusion. If one can cleanse these stains on the mind, then one may overcome all harmful thoughts and emotions.

Today's Date:

This quote inspires the following thoughts in me:

This quote inspires me to take these actions today:

(Before bedtime) I accomplished these actions today:

"Maintain a state of balance between physical activity and inner serenity, like a lute whose strings are finely tuned." - The Buddha

In today's fast-paced society, it is all too common to be in a state of constant motion with little space for inner serenity. In order to find our balance, we need to take time every day for physical activity and also find moments throughout the day when we can focus on being still. Being in a state of balance between these two will be key to maintaining what The Buddha called The Middle Path.

Today's Date:

This quote inspires the following thoughts in me:

This quote inspires me to take these actions today:

(Before bedtime) I accomplished these actions today:

"I am a finger pointing to the moon. Don't look at me; look at the moon." - The Buddha

The Buddha didn't want anyone to worship him. He was just a man who attained enlightenment; he didn't pretend to be a god. He wanted us to know enlightenment is available to each one of us, when we follow the path his teachings point towards. Focus on the moon!

Today's Date:

This quote inspires the following thoughts in me:

This quote inspires me to take these actions today:

(Before bedtime) I accomplished these actions today:

"When things are going well, be mindful of adversity. When prosperous, be mindful of poverty. When loved, be mindful of thoughtfulness. When respected, be mindful of humility." - The Buddha

The Buddha taught that The Middle Path keeps us grounded in the moment. We don't allow our emotions to swing to and fro like a pendulum. Whatever is happening in our lives, we strive to stop the pendulum from swinging. We strive to stay in the middle of all our emotions, always balanced, always aware of the possibility of change.

Today's Date:

This quote inspires the following thoughts in me:

This quote inspires me to take these actions today:

(Before bedtime) I accomplished these actions today:

"Better it is to live one day seeing the rise and fall of things than to live a hundred years without ever seeing the rise and fall of things." - The Buddha

Is it possible that a person who lives but a short time may be more fulfilled and happy than one who lives for hundred years? Of course, the answer is yes, if the person with the shorter lifespan lives fully in each moment. Isn't it better to fully experience the splendor of life than to live a long life without knowing the wonder of life?

Today's Date:

This quote inspires the following thoughts in me:

This quote inspires me to take these actions today:

(Before bedtime) I accomplished these actions today:

"If you find no one to support you on the spiritual path, walk alone." - The Buddha

What happens when you find no one around you to support your meditation and spiritual practice? You can continue to grow on your spiritual path even if you are completely alone - just like The Buddha did. All the answers are within you at this very moment. Don't wait for a teacher to tell you the way. Just begin to search within.

Today's Date:

This quote inspires the following thoughts in me:

This quote inspires me to take these actions today:

(Before bedtime) I accomplished these actions today:

"To support mother and father, to cherish wife and child and to have a simple livelihood; this is the best of life." - The Buddha

A life in which we care for our loved ones, do beneficial and honest work, and acquire just what we need to live a simple life is one of the best recipe for happiness. We're happier when we know we're making a difference in people's lives and aren't an obstacle in their paths.

Today's Date:

This quote inspires the following thoughts in me:

This quote inspires me to take these actions today:

(Before bedtime) I accomplished these actions today:

"It is in the nature of things that joy arises in a person free from remorse." - The Buddha

While it can be helpful to recognize that mistakes happen and that we are human, feeling forever guilty for past mistakes doesn't do us any good. When we allow ourselves to feel guilty for past mistakes, we allow ourselves to be stuck in a place where there's no escape. The solution isn't always easy, but it starts with learning how to forgive yourself and move on.

Today's Date:

This quote inspires the following thoughts in me:

This quote inspires me to take these actions today:

(Before bedtime) I accomplished these actions today:

"When it hurts, observe. Life is trying to teach you something." - The Buddha

For a true learner, life is a classroom. It's a time for moments of discovery and insight that other people might not notice or understand the impact of. In every disappointment, there is an opportunity for learning how to live more fully, with less pain - to be our truest selves.

Today's Date:

This quote inspires the following thoughts in me:

This quote inspires me to take these actions today:

(Before bedtime) I accomplished these actions today:

"All life is temporary. Why worry about anything that's only temporary?" - The Buddha

Nothing in this world is permanent. Good and bad things happen and then they're gone. You can't do anything about it, so why worry about anything that's only temporary? Life is a gift and it should be cherished, not feared. If you live in the moment, you will never have regrets when someone or something passes away or moves on to another life stage or stage in life.

Today's Date:

This quote inspires the following thoughts in me:

This quote inspires me to take these actions today:

(Before bedtime) I accomplished these actions today:

"You are a seeker. Delight in the mastery of your hands and your feet, of your words and your thoughts." - The Buddha

Seek and search out those things that make you happy, those things that bring excitement to your life. And the best part is that, as a seeker, no matter how far or how deep into your journey of self-discovery you go, there's always something else waiting for you to discover.

Today's Date:

This quote inspires the following thoughts in me:

This quote inspires me to take these actions today:

(Before bedtime) I accomplished these actions today:

"You must love yourself before you love another. By accepting yourself and fully being what you are, your simple presence can make others happy."
- The Buddha

The way you feel about yourself has even more of an impact on how others see you than the other way around. It is not selfish or narcissistic to care first for yourself. It will help create a more positive environment for everyone around you.

Today's Date:

This quote inspires the following thoughts in me:

This quote inspires me to take these actions today:

(Before bedtime) I accomplished these actions today:

"Our sorrows and wounds are healed only when we touch them with compassion." - The Buddha

I know it may sound easy, but touch your wounds with self-compassion and they will heal themselves. But, for most of us, the wounds seem to reoccur and we don't understand why. If we can stop denying ourselves love and accept that we are worthy of love on our own, then maybe the pain would lessen.

Today's Date:

This quote inspires the following thoughts in me:

This quote inspires me to take these actions today:

(Before bedtime) I accomplished these actions today:

"Until he has unconditional and unbiased love for all beings, man will not find peace." - The Buddha

Unconditional love is the ability to love someone despite their flaws or transgressions. It is not dependent on anything they do or say because you know they are doing the best they can. Peace and harmony can only be attained when each and every human being loves and accepts themselves and others for who they are. Only when we have unconditional love for all beings, regardless of circumstance , will we find peace within ourselves.

Today's Date:

This quote inspires the following thoughts in me:

This quote inspires me to take these actions today:

(Before bedtime) I accomplished these actions today:

"Life is a circle of happiness, sadness, hard times, and good times. If you are going through hard times, have faith that good times are on the way." - The Buddha

In life, there will be good times and bad, joyful moments and those that make us cry. Sometimes we feel as if everything is going our way, but other times we don't know how we'll make it through the day. The middle way of these extremes can be difficult to find. For those with a strong sense of self, the answer may come easier - an inner peace with oneself is a form of resistance to all that life throws at us.

Today's Date:

This quote inspires the following thoughts in me:

This quote inspires me to take these actions today:

(Before bedtime) I accomplished these actions today:

"You will not be punished for your anger; you will be punished by your anger." - The Buddha

Anger is a natural response to hurt or injustice. It's something we often feel, and might even seek out as a way of coping with the stressors in our lives. The problem is that anger can be so all-consuming, it becomes hard to see beyond the emotion—and this is what causes it to turn inward, causing us more pain than the person or object we meant to direct it towards.

Today's Date:

This quote inspires the following thoughts in me:

This quote inspires me to take these actions today:

(Before bedtime) I accomplished these actions today:

"Even loss and betrayal can bring us awakening."
- The Buddha

Daily, we face the many emotions that come with the release of our attachments, which are often experienced as loss. Sometimes these emotions feel like betrayal because to release an attachment means to detach from something or someone that felt so close and was so dear. But this is not brokenness. This is not a sign of failure. It's actually a sign of being present in life, being able to adjust to change, open heartedly embracing what life brings us.

Today's Date:

This quote inspires the following thoughts in me:

This quote inspires me to take these actions today:

(Before bedtime) I accomplished these actions today:

"Let none find fault with others; let none see the omissions and commissions of others. But let one see one's own acts, done and undone." - The Buddha

Fault-finding and criticism go hand in hand. When we believe someone has done something wrong, it's difficult to resist the urge to point out their mistakes or yell at them about how they could have done better. But what if we were to shift our focus from finding other people's faults and instead found fault with ourselves?

Today's Date:

This quote inspires the following thoughts in me:

This quote inspires me to take these actions today:

(Before bedtime) I accomplished these actions today:

"As you walk and eat and travel, be where you are.
Otherwise you will miss most of your life."
- The Buddha

The common fast-paced lifestyle we live, and the tendency to be constantly on the go has led us to miss out on a lot in life. We spend so much of our time thinking about what is happening elsewhere and not a moment to enjoy the beauty of the present. We wander through life with our heads down, looking at our phones, focused on any number of things that are not actually happening.

Today's Date:

This quote inspires the following thoughts in me:

This quote inspires me to take these actions today:

(Before bedtime) I accomplished these actions today:

"Pain in life is inevitable but suffering is not. Pain is what the world does to you, suffering is what you do to yourself." - The Buddha

You have the choice to be free from suffering, but it may take courage and time to find your way out. The journey begins not by eliminating pain or feelings, but by looking at them differently. With continuous practice of changing your perspective of life we can all move beyond suffering and into a more peaceful state of being.

Today's Date:

This quote inspires the following thoughts in me:

This quote inspires me to take these actions today:

(Before bedtime) I accomplished these actions today:

"Walking with a friend in the dark is better than walking alone in the light." - The Buddha

When it comes to having a friend in your life, there is no substitute for the feeling of support and love that comes from being with someone who understands you. In a world full of hectic schedules and tough decisions, nothing can replace the comfort and security that comes from someone who has walked with you through it all. It does not matter where you walk together: in the light or in the dark. What matters is that you take each step together.

Today's Date:

This quote inspires the following thoughts in me:

This quote inspires me to take these actions today:

(Before bedtime) I accomplished these actions today:

"I do not dispute with the world; rather it is the world that disputes with me." - The Buddha

You have choice in all things. If someone attempts to pull you into an argument, you can choose a path of peace instead. Your calm and compassion will win any argument. Why not move the conversation in a new direction? Or just offer a smile and move on?

Today's Date:

This quote inspires the following thoughts in me:

This quote inspires me to take these actions today:

(Before bedtime) I accomplished these actions today:

"You yourself must strive. The Buddha only points the way." - The Buddha

A great teacher doesn't do the work for her students. She sets them on the correct path of discovery, and frees them to uncover the truth for themselves.

Today's Date:

This quote inspires the following thoughts in me:

This quote inspires me to take these actions today:

(Before bedtime) I accomplished these actions today:

"Purity or impurity depends on oneself. No one can purify another." - The Buddha

You must struggle with your own faults and not expect someone else to fix them. Many people have a tendency to avoid things that they don't want to do or that they struggle with because of a lack of self-compassion. Rather than dealing with the issue head-on, people will often create excuses and find ways to dodge their responsibilities. In doing so, these people are living in denial instead of facing what is really going on.

Today's Date:

This quote inspires the following thoughts in me:

This quote inspires me to take these actions today:

(Before bedtime) I accomplished these actions today:

"The one who has conquered himself is a far greater hero than he who has defeated a thousand times a thousand men." - The Buddha

Knowing the self well, being self-compassionate, and taking responsibility for oneself are all qualities of a person that deserve to be celebrated. A self-aware, self-compassionate, self-responsible person has more to be proud of than the person who chooses a life without introspection. When one is aware of themselves and their actions, they are on the path to experiencing their life fully.

Today's Date:

This quote inspires the following thoughts in me:

This quote inspires me to take these actions today:

(Before bedtime) I accomplished these actions today:

"Every morning we are born again. What we do today is what matters most." - The Buddha

Some people live with regret and each day is a struggle to make up for what they missed during their past. Others live in fear and fear what the future may hold. Yet others live with guilt and never feel like they're good enough. These mindsets restrict us from living the life we want, not only for ourselves but also for those around us. Every morning, it's time to start fresh. What you do today is what matters most, so embrace the day with open arms and take care of what needs taking care of.

Today's Date:

This quote inspires the following thoughts in me:

This quote inspires me to take these actions today:

(Before bedtime) I accomplished these actions today:

"Our life is shaped by our mind; we become what we think. Joy follows a pure thought like a shadow that never leaves." - The Buddha

Life can be rough. We all have moments where we feel like life is just too much and that happiness is elusive or completely out of reach. When we understand and believe that our thoughts shape what happens in our world, however, we find it easier to find joy and happiness in the smallest of things. Let go of the rough moments, won't you?

Today's Date:

This quote inspires the following thoughts in me:

This quote inspires me to take these actions today:

(Before bedtime) I accomplished these actions today:

"Your mind is a powerful thing. When you start to filter it with positive thoughts your life will start to change." - The Buddha

You have the power to control your own happiness, simply by choosing to approach your life with love and self-compassion. What's holding you back? The list of repetitive negative thoughts in our brains tell us that the outside world is to blame for our unhappiness. The truth is, you are responsible for your happiness. Will you try something new?

Today's Date:

This quote inspires the following thoughts in me:

This quote inspires me to take these actions today:

(Before bedtime) I accomplished these actions today:

"You are far from the end of your journey. The way is not in the sky. The way is in the heart. See how you love." - The Buddha

When you long for the journey to be over, it is telling you that there is still more to learn. You are not lost, but on your way home. Life is not about reaching an end, but it's about how you live each day of your life. Happiness and joy are found in the present moment, not in some far off destination.

Today's Date:

This quote inspires the following thoughts in me:

This quote inspires me to take these actions today:

(Before bedtime) I accomplished these actions today:

"You don't need someone to complete you; you only need someone to accept you completely."
- The Buddha

Your relationship with another person is not meant to make you whole or make up for the things you lack. In fact, many people find their most fulfilling relationships when they can be 100% themselves without fear of judgement. It is all about accepting the other person completely and knowing that even if you are not perfect, you will still be loved by them unconditionally.

Today's Date:

This quote inspires the following thoughts in me:

This quote inspires me to take these actions today:

(Before bedtime) I accomplished these actions today:

"The way to happiness is: keep your heart free from hate, your mind from worry. Live simply, give much. Fill your life with love. Do as you would be done by."
- The Buddha

What if living a happy life is in fact simpler than we ever imagined? What if the answers that we have been seeking are right in front of us? The answers that will teach us how to live with kindness, self-compassion and love? What would happen if, instead of focusing on the "end game," we focused on this moment?

Today's Date:

<u>This quote inspires the following thoughts in me:</u>

<u>This quote inspires me to take these actions today:</u>

<u>(Before bedtime) I accomplished these actions today:</u>

"Your suffering is my suffering and your happiness is my happiness." - The Buddha

Everything in this world is interconnected. From the small to the great, from the near to the far, everything has a link with each other. The relationships that exist in this world are like an intricate web which cannot be separated or broken into pieces. When you know this, you understand how everything you say and do has an impact on the entire world.

Today's Date:

This quote inspires the following thoughts in me:

This quote inspires me to take these actions today:

(Before bedtime) I accomplished these actions today:

"When a bird is alive, it eats ants. When the bird is dead, ants eat the bird. Time and circumstances can change at any time." - The Buddha

Nothing in life is permanent. Everything in life is transitory. Accept that change is coming and live fully in this moment. Your happiness depends on it.

Today's Date:

This quote inspires the following thoughts in me:

This quote inspires me to take these actions today:

(Before bedtime) I accomplished these actions today:

"Do not look for a sanctuary in anyone except yourself." - The Buddha

If you're struggling to find happiness in your life, don't look for it outside of yourself. The answer is inside of you and can be found by looking deep within. You cannot depend on material things or other people's praise for you to have a happy life because if they disappear, so will your imagined happiness.

Today's Date:

This quote inspires the following thoughts in me:

This quote inspires me to take these actions today:

(Before bedtime) I accomplished these actions today:

"When an evil-doer, seeing you practise goodness, comes and maliciously insults you, you should patiently endure it and not feel angry with him, for the evil-doer is insulting himself by trying to insult you."
- The Buddha

It is the natural human tendency to react when we feel insulted, but it is important to remember that an insult may not be what it seems. Even if someone is trying to hurt you, they are usually projecting their own pain onto you and should be pitied for this. React with loving-kindness, and change them.

Today's Date:

This quote inspires the following thoughts in me:

This quote inspires me to take these actions today:

(Before bedtime) I accomplished these actions today:

"A fool learns nothing from a wise man; but a wise man learns much from a fool." - The Buddha

It is the fool, in his ignorance, who cannot see the error of his own ways. The wise man, being already knowledgeable in life, can easily see what the fool does not. Pay attention to those around you, and judge for yourself who is wise.

Today's Date:

This quote inspires the following thoughts in me:

This quote inspires me to take these actions today:

(Before bedtime) I accomplished these actions today:

"All beings tremble before violence. All love life. All fear death. See yourself in others. Then whom can you hurt? What harm can you do?" - The Buddha

We are all connected in the cycle of life. Whether it is through our love for others, or fear of death. It's possible to see beyond our own needs and look at the world around us with compassion and understanding instead of judgement.

Today's Date:

This quote inspires the following thoughts in me:

This quote inspires me to take these actions today:

(Before bedtime) I accomplished these actions today:

"As a mountain is unshaken by the wind, so the heart of a wise person is unmoved by all the changes on this earth." - The Buddha

How does the wise person's heart remain unmoved by any changes? Is it fortitude, or is it enlightenment? What are the foundations of this fortitude? It is wisdom, which leads to fortitude and enlightenment. Wisdom comes from life experience and understanding.

Today's Date:

This quote inspires the following thoughts in me:

This quote inspires me to take these actions today:

(Before bedtime) I accomplished these actions today:

"Nothing can harm you as much as your own thoughts unguarded." - The Buddha

Many people don't realize the power inside their own minds. Thoughts are constantly running through our minds, but if we're not aware of them, they can take control of our reactions and emotions. What do you think about your thoughts? Do they help you with your life or tear you down?

Today's Date:

This quote inspires the following thoughts in me:

This quote inspires me to take these actions today:

(Before bedtime) I accomplished these actions today:

"I will not look at another's life intent on finding fault."
- The Buddha

I will not look at another's life intent on finding fault, but try to only find the good. I will not take joy in someone's pain, but find pleasure in their happiness. I will live my life understanding that all things happen for a reason and the urge to criticize another rises in me, I will ask myself, "What do I see in myself that would cause me to criticize them?"

Today's Date:

This quote inspires the following thoughts in me:

This quote inspires me to take these actions today:

(Before bedtime) I accomplished these actions today:

"As you travel though life, offer good wishes to each being you meet." - The Buddha

Every day, people meet new people, old friends, and acquaintances. Status, wealth, race, religion - none of these things matter when we offer good wishes to the beings we meet. Good wishes are a way to share love and happiness with others in our lives. People often say that life is like an eternal journey and we should always be mindful of the people we come across and offer goodness and kindness to them because they may not get another chance.

Today's Date:

This quote inspires the following thoughts in me:

This quote inspires me to take these actions today:

(Before bedtime) I accomplished these actions today:

"Be greatly aware of the present." - The Buddha

Life is very uncertain. One moment it's there, the next, it's gone. Be mindful of the present because it is all that really exists. Spend your time doing what you love in this moment, while you can.

Today's Date:

This quote inspires the following thoughts in me:

This quote inspires me to take these actions today:

(Before bedtime) I accomplished these actions today:

"Hatred does not cease by hatred, but only by love; this is the eternal rule." - The Buddha

We can only find true peace and happiness when we use the power of our love to connect with the world. Don't waste a moment on hate, either from within you or from without. Love is at the center of your happiness.

Today's Date:

This quote inspires the following thoughts in me:

This quote inspires me to take these actions today:

(Before bedtime) I accomplished these actions today:

"We will develop and cultivate the liberation of mind by loving-kindness, make it our vehicle, make it our basis, stabilize it, exercise ourselves in it, and fully perfect it." - The Buddha

We have all experienced moments when we are not present or are caught up in our own thoughts, which often leads to anger, frustration, annoyance, or other negative feelings. By the cultivation of lovingkindness we can nurture a sense of inner warmth and compassion that helps us overcome the mental disturbances that keep us from being fully present.

Today's Date:

This quote inspires the following thoughts in me:

This quote inspires me to take these actions today:

(Before bedtime) I accomplished these actions today:

"Do what makes you happy. Be with who makes you smile. Laugh as much as you breathe. Love as long as you live." - The Buddha

Living in a world of problems, it is easy to lose sight of what is important in life. Happiness is just one decision away, so be sure that the decisions you make are the best for yourself and your loved ones around you. What an easy formula for living life fully!

Today's Date:

This quote inspires the following thoughts in me:

This quote inspires me to take these actions today:

(Before bedtime) I accomplished these actions today:

"All beings wish for happiness, so extend your compassion to all." - The Buddha

By sharing the loving-kindness and compassion in your heart with everyone you encounter, you are fulfilling the wish of every person to find happiness. What greater gift can you give?

Today's Date:

This quote inspires the following thoughts in me:

This quote inspires me to take these actions today:

(Before bedtime) I accomplished these actions today:

"Not even death can wipe out our good deeds."
- The Buddha

Everyone leaves a legacy behind, whether they intend to or not. We all have a self-imposed responsibility to ensure that the things we do and say will leave a positive trace on the lives of those around us. There are many ways for us to work towards making that happen, which is why it's so important for us to pause and take stock from time to time. Reflecting on what we've lived through can help us define what we want to be remembered for.

Today's Date:

This quote inspires the following thoughts in me:

This quote inspires me to take these actions today:

(Before bedtime) I accomplished these actions today:

"Before enlightenment; chop wood, carry water. After enlightenment; chop wood, carry water."
- The Buddha

If you achieve enlightenment, what will change about you? Will you suddenly be without challenges? Will you stop experiencing hunger or thirst? Or will you continue to do everything that must be done each day, but with a smile on your face, and loving-kindness and compassion in your heart for everyone along the way?

Today's Date:

This quote inspires the following thoughts in me:

This quote inspires me to take these actions today:

(Before bedtime) I accomplished these actions today:

"Fools wait for a lucky day but everyday is lucky for an industrious person." - The Buddha

Happiness and success comes to those who work hard for it. There is no sense in sitting around waiting for all that you wish for to just magically appear. Have the intention, do the work, and it will come.

Today's Date:

This quote inspires the following thoughts in me:

This quote inspires me to take these actions today:

(Before bedtime) I accomplished these actions today:

"By your own folly you will be brought as low as your worst enemy wishes." - The Buddha

While it may seem like the world is out to get you at times, no one can hurt you unless you allow them to. You have a choice to be happy and positive in the face adversity or dwell on the negatives that come your way. What will you choose today?

Today's Date:

This quote inspires the following thoughts in me:

This quote inspires me to take these actions today:

(Before bedtime) I accomplished these actions today:

"Nothing is forever except change."
- The Buddha

Every single moment in time is fleeting, and nothing stays the same for more than a few seconds. There are so many things to be happy about because of this. Change gives opportunities for new beginnings, interesting twists, and stepping into something completely foreign. If you let change come without resisting it, then it will be an enriching experience that will bring happiness to your life.

Today's Date:

This quote inspires the following thoughts in me:

This quote inspires me to take these actions today:

(Before bedtime) I accomplished these actions today:

"Craving brings pain; craving brings fear. If you do not yield to craving, you will be free from pain and fear." - The Buddha

Attachment to and desire for things that you don't have cause you to suffer. Give up these things and you will be free from the pain and fear not having what you crave brings.

Today's Date:

This quote inspires the following thoughts in me:

This quote inspires me to take these actions today:

(Before bedtime) I accomplished these actions today:

"All wrong-doing arises because of mind. If mind is transformed can wrong-doing remain?"
- The Buddha

We create our own suffering and happiness through our thoughts and actions. We don't have to do anything in particular in order for this to happen, simply recognize when we are caught up in our thoughts and choose the most wholesome thought or action.

Today's Date:

This quote inspires the following thoughts in me:

This quote inspires me to take these actions today:

(Before bedtime) I accomplished these actions today:

"Do not speak – unless it improves on silence."
- The Buddha

We all know people who try to be the smartest ones in the room, always expressing their opinion on this or that. But we actually hold the most respect for the person who saves her thought for the moment when it will have the most impact. Which person would you rather be?

Today's Date:

This quote inspires the following thoughts in me:

This quote inspires me to take these actions today:

(Before bedtime) I accomplished these actions today:

"Do not overlook tiny good actions, thinking they are of no benefit; even tiny drops of water, in the end, will fill a huge vessel. Do not overlook negative actions merely because they are small; however small a spark may be, it can burn down a haystack as big as a mountain." - The Buddha

The total sum of our good and bad actions throughout our lifetime will leave an impact on the world, no matter how large or small each action was. Knowing this, doesn't it make sense to constantly ask yourself if want you are doing in this moment is helpful or hurtful?

Today's Date:

This quote inspires the following thoughts in me:

This quote inspires me to take these actions today:

(Before bedtime) I accomplished these actions today:

"Do not think of how big the universe is, it will merely hurt your head. " - The Buddha

Instead, be fully aware of what is happening around you and within you, and discover the happiness that fills your being.

Today's Date:

This quote inspires the following thoughts in me:

This quote inspires me to take these actions today:

(Before bedtime) I accomplished these actions today:

"Just as the great ocean has one taste, the taste of salt, so also this teaching and discipline has one taste, the taste of liberation." - The Buddha

The taste of liberation, according to the Buddha, is detachment. This means viewing everything as equal and not attaching to anything. Liberation is achieved by eliminating all attachment, or desire. Our desires are the cause of suffering; therefore, achieving this state of detachment is necessary for enlightenment.

Today's Date:

This quote inspires the following thoughts in me:

This quote inspires me to take these actions today:

(Before bedtime) I accomplished these actions today:

"The trouble is, you think you have time."
- The Buddha

Not one of us is guaranteed another day, let alone another minute. Shouldn't we be spending our precious time focused on this moment, rather than hanging onto regrets, or worrying about the future? And instead of spending our time worrying about how others perceive us or fear of potential failure, why not spend the limited time we have focusing on possibilities in this moment?

Today's Date:

This quote inspires the following thoughts in me:

This quote inspires me to take these actions today:

(Before bedtime) I accomplished these actions today:

"Even if everyone else is not doing good, I alone will. Even if everyone else is doing wrong, I alone will not."
- The Buddha

Each of us must decide at some point what values we hold dear enough to live by, no matter the circumstances. Sometimes it's difficult to not go along with the crowd, but the strength to do the right thing in every situation grows each time we exercise it.

Today's Date:

This quote inspires the following thoughts in me:

This quote inspires me to take these actions today:

(Before bedtime) I accomplished these actions today:

"Flower and thorn are in the same stem."
- The Buddha

We all have good times and bad times. But surprisingly, these two things are not opposites. Flowers and thorns grow side by side in the same stem. The flowers bloom with beauty, while the thorn prickles with pain. Humans can experience both at once, and we can learn from this paradoxical example of nature that sometimes you need to experience something painful to get something beautiful.

Today's Date:

This quote inspires the following thoughts in me:

This quote inspires me to take these actions today:

(Before bedtime) I accomplished these actions today:

"Give thanks for what had been given to you, however little. Be pure, never falter."
- The Buddha

Every blessing you receive in this life, no matter how small, is something to be grateful for. Sometimes these may not appear to be blessing at first, but if you continue to remain in this moment and allow yourself to be open to the possibilities, even a painful event can be learned from. Stay mindful.

Today's Date:

This quote inspires the following thoughts in me:

This quote inspires me to take these actions today:

(Before bedtime) I accomplished these actions today:

"Give the people – confidence. Give the people – delight. Give the people – hope. Give the people – the best."
- The Buddha

How do you help other people to be their best selves? We've all had family members, friends and co-workers or bosses who use negativity to get what they want. Does it work in the long run? How do you interact with those you love and those you work with? Is it always from a place of love and compassion?

Today's Date:

This quote inspires the following thoughts in me:

This quote inspires me to take these actions today:

(Before bedtime) I accomplished these actions today:

"Know well what holds you back, and what moves you forward." - The Buddha

What you resist has a tendency to persist. if we don't know what's holding us back, we can't find our way forward. But this doesn't mean we simply accept all obstacles as given. Our thoughts and attitudes determine how much effect any particular obstacle has on us. Once we figure out what holds us back and stop feeding those thoughts, we're free to move forward and achieve our goals.

Today's Date:

This quote inspires the following thoughts in me:

This quote inspires me to take these actions today:

(Before bedtime) I accomplished these actions today:

"Stop, stop. Do not speak. The ultimate truth is not even to think." - The Buddha

People often say that their mind is racing and they can't stop thinking, but what if the answer to this is not more thought? What if the answer is to stop and let your brain fill with silence and stillness?

Today's Date:

This quote inspires the following thoughts in me:

This quote inspires me to take these actions today:

(Before bedtime) I accomplished these actions today:

"Love in the past is only a memory. Love in the future is only a fantasy. True love lives in the here and now."
- The Buddha

Love is what we all want, whether it be in the past or in the future. We all want that one person to love us just for who we are, to support us in what we do, and cheer us on when we're feeling down. Yet how can anyone find true love when so wrapped up in the events of the past and the wishes for the future? True love lives inside of you, right here and right now, doesn't it?

Today's Date:

This quote inspires the following thoughts in me:

This quote inspires me to take these actions today:

(Before bedtime) I accomplished these actions today:

"He who never thinks of anything as 'mine' does not feel the lack of anything: he is never worried by a sense of loss." - The Buddha

Each of us has items that we treasure and assign an emotional value to. However, what if we didn't feel the need to cling to these things, and instead let go? It may be hard to imagine a life where we don't attach ourselves to anything, but in Buddhism there is a concept called 'Anatmavada'. The idea of Anatmavada is that all things exist as part of a web of interconnectedness. There is not "yours," and not "mine," only "ours."

Today's Date:

This quote inspires the following thoughts in me:

This quote inspires me to take these actions today:

(Before bedtime) I accomplished these actions today:

"If you don't see God in the next person you meet, look no further." - The Buddha

Each of us has that of God inside of us, in equal amounts. We are all connected, and therefore, all the same. If you are not able to see that another person has the same capacity for kindness, love, and compassion in her that you have, you must not see it in yourself either.

Today's Date:

This quote inspires the following thoughts in me:

This quote inspires me to take these actions today:

(Before bedtime) I accomplished these actions today:

"Believe nothing, no matter where you read it, or who said it, no matter if I have said it, unless it agrees with your own reason and your own common sense."
- The Buddha

Each of us should listen carefully to our own heart and should use our own intelligence as a way to decipher truth. If we allow ourselves to blindly follow everything we hear without seeking truth for ourselves, we may be left believing in something that is untrue.

Today's Date:

This quote inspires the following thoughts in me:

This quote inspires me to take these actions today:

(Before bedtime) I accomplished these actions today:

"If you're depressed, you're living in the past. If you're anxious, you're living in the future. If you're at peace, you're living in the present." - The Buddha

We are often so caught up in the past or future that we forget to live in the present. But what if, by living in the present, you were able to be content with your life and embrace happiness?

Today's Date:

This quote inspires the following thoughts in me:

This quote inspires me to take these actions today:

(Before bedtime) I accomplished these actions today:

"Don't treat people as bad as they are; treat them as good as you are." - The Buddha

It costs you nothing to treat every person you meet with good intentions, even if they are poor or rude or unpleasant. If someone is in need, be kind to them instead of treating them poorly. If someone is rude, don't ignore the behavior and instead consider what's going on in their life that has them acting this way. Maybe they actually need your help.

Today's Date:

This quote inspires the following thoughts in me:

This quote inspires me to take these actions today:

(Before bedtime) I accomplished these actions today:

"Before you speak, let your words pass through three gates: Is it true? Is it necessary? Is it kind?"
- The Buddha

Let these be the gatekeepers to what will come out of your mouth. If you cannot answer yes to all three, then rethink your words before they make their way out of your mouth and into someone else's life. Before long, you will find yourself listening more and talking less, but when you do speak, every one will listen closely.

Today's Date:

This quote inspires the following thoughts in me:

This quote inspires me to take these actions today:

(Before bedtime) I accomplished these actions today:

"Your body is precious. It is our vehicle for awakening. Treat it with care." - The Buddha

We must be as careful with taking care of our bodies as we are with taking care of our minds. One doesn't exist without the other. Some people prefer the gym to the library, and completely ignore the growth of their minds. Others prefer the life of the mind, but let their bodies go without proper diet and exercise. The middle path tells us that we must do both to be at our best. Where do you fall on this spectrum?

Today's Date:

This quote inspires the following thoughts in me:

This quote inspires me to take these actions today:

(Before bedtime) I accomplished these actions today:

"There are only two days in the year that nothing can be done. One is called yesterday and the other is called tomorrow, so today is the right day to love, believe, do and mostly live." - The Buddha

There is no better time than today to forget about yesterday and any worries for tomorrow. Live in the moment with no regrets for what has passed and with no worries about what is yet to come. Life is an unpredictable journey that requires one to live each day as it comes without worrying about the future or regretting the past. One should be thankful for every minute of every day, as they are all a great opportunity for happiness and contentment.

Today's Date:

This quote inspires the following thoughts in me:

This quote inspires me to take these actions today:

(Before bedtime) I accomplished these actions today:

"Through effort, you will cross any raging flood, through energy you will pass any sorrow."
- The Buddha

When you have found the center of your happiness, and can live in the present moment without regret or fear, you will be able to conquer whatever challenges come into your life. You have the strength and power to overcome anything, if only you would believe it.

Today's Date:

This quote inspires the following thoughts in me:

This quote inspires me to take these actions today:

(Before bedtime) I accomplished these actions today:

"Inner freedom is not guided by our efforts; it comes from seeing what is true." - The Buddha

Cultivating inner freedom is not about striving to "be" free. It's about seeing what is true so it becomes easier to act on what we see. Most of us are ruled by thoughts and feelings that are not our own. They come from an aspect of our mind that observes everything but is not attached to anything. Inner freedom comes with clarity into this observer-mind, which means having less judgment about people and things around us.

Today's Date:

This quote inspires the following thoughts in me:

This quote inspires me to take these actions today:

(Before bedtime) I accomplished these actions today:

"It is impossible to underestimate the significance of your the choices you make today." - The Buddha

How many times have you made a choice in your life without thinking the full consequences of the decision would unfold? Regardless of how small that decision may seem, it will most likely have consequences down the line. Listen to your heart and choose wisely, because the smallest decision you make today may have huge consequences tomorrow.

Today's Date:

This quote inspires the following thoughts in me:

This quote inspires me to take these actions today:

(Before bedtime) I accomplished these actions today:

"Joy comes not through possession or ownership but through a wise and loving heart."
- The Buddha

Where ever we go we are bombarded with advertising telling us that happiness can only happen for us when we possess this product or that service. But the key to finding true happiness starts with one's self. True happiness comes from within and it can be found by putting others before oneself, through healthy living practices, and by being grateful for the things that one already has.

Today's Date:

This quote inspires the following thoughts in me:

This quote inspires me to take these actions today:

(Before bedtime) I accomplished these actions today:

"Kindness is giving others happiness. Compassion is removing others' bitterness. Joy is freeing others from suffering." - The Buddha

We've all heard the phrase "pay it forward." This means we give kind deeds to other people and encourage them to pass it on and do something nice for someone else. The idea is that by spreading kindness and compassion, you will be able to make the world a better place. What could be better than helping others discover the joy and happiness that exists in abundance within them?

Today's Date:

This quote inspires the following thoughts in me:

This quote inspires me to take these actions today:

(Before bedtime) I accomplished these actions today:

"May I hold myself in compassion." - The Buddha

Throughout the history of the world, there have been a select few who have reached enlightenment and been able to teach others how to live in peace with themselves. But even these enlightened beings, such as the Buddha, still had to practice what they preached every day. He knew that self-compassion was the key to it all. This is a challenge for each of us - to hold ourselves tightly in self-compassion at all times.

Today's Date:

This quote inspires the following thoughts in me:

This quote inspires me to take these actions today:

(Before bedtime) I accomplished these actions today:

"Seeker, empty the boat, lighten the load, be free of craving and judgment and hatred, and feel the joy of the way." - The Buddha

There is a feeling of inner peace and happiness that comes from living in the present moment. There is little to no craving for past or future moments, and we are free to enjoy the present moment for what it is. This state of mind, known as "mindfulness," requires letting go of judgment and hatred against oneself or others.

Today's Date:

This quote inspires the following thoughts in me:

This quote inspires me to take these actions today:

(Before bedtime) I accomplished these actions today:

"Serenity comes when you trade expectations for acceptance." - The Buddha

The only way to find serenity is by accepting life as it is, no matter how uncomfortable. Our minds are always looking for ways to make the best of things, but what happens when you can't? You need to realize that this is normal and embrace life's unpredictability. The key to happiness lies in your ability to accept what life throws at you.

Today's Date:

This quote inspires the following thoughts in me:

This quote inspires me to take these actions today:

(Before bedtime) I accomplished these actions today:

"Stay centered, do not overstretch. Extend from your center, return to your center."
- The Buddha

Mindfulness is centeredness, focus of attention on the current activity, and awareness of one's thoughts and feelings without judgment or critique. When we're mindful, we're open and aware to the present moment. We might be setting up for dinner or washing dishes, but we're aware of our thoughts and feelings as they arise. This awareness is what sets us apart from the past and future as we live in the present.

Today's Date:

This quote inspires the following thoughts in me:

This quote inspires me to take these actions today:

(Before bedtime) I accomplished these actions today:

297

"The end of desire is the end of sorrow." - The Buddha

When we want something, we often crave for it and think about it all the time. We let the desire control us and take over our lives. When we stop desiring anything and accept what is, we will be free from sorrow and suffering in the world.

Today's Date:

This quote inspires the following thoughts in me:

This quote inspires me to take these actions today:

(Before bedtime) I accomplished these actions today:

"The more fully we give our energy, the more it returns to us." - The Buddha

Karma is a principle of causality where intent and actions can have consequences. The principle of karma is the driving force behind the array of life's experiences. In other words, our thoughts and actions will always return to us in some form for better or for worse. Knowing this, why would we ever choose to do something unkind?

Today's Date:

This quote inspires the following thoughts in me:

This quote inspires me to take these actions today:

(Before bedtime) I accomplished these actions today:

"The right time to show your good character is when you are pestered by someone weaker than you."
- The Buddha

It's easy to belittle a weaker person, but when instead we are kind and compassionate, we show our true strength. We all know the feeling of being put down by someone who appears stronger or more confident than we do; it can feel like an attack on our whole identity and leave us feeling hopeless and defeated. How much better is it to demonstrate the true way to them, with kindness?

Today's Date:

This quote inspires the following thoughts in me:

This quote inspires me to take these actions today:

(Before bedtime) I accomplished these actions today:

"Stop trying to calm the storm. Calm yourself, and the storm will pass." - The Buddha

Many of us worry that we may not be able to control our emotions or reactions, especially when it comes to certain triggers like anger, sadness, and frustration. We should focus instead on the moment, and seek our center. When we accomplish this we are able to see life for how it really is - transitory. This way we grow internally strong, and can outlast any storm.

Today's Date:

This quote inspires the following thoughts in me:

This quote inspires me to take these actions today:

(Before bedtime) I accomplished these actions today:

"There's a treasury full of jade and jewels; It is in you.
Don't go searching far from home for it - it's here."
- The Buddha

All the happiness you seek is inside you, if you would only realize it. You may live a life of luxury, and be miserable. You may live a life of poverty, and be joyful. The treasure is inside you. What will you do today to seek it out?

Today's Date:

This quote inspires the following thoughts in me:

This quote inspires me to take these actions today:

(Before bedtime) I accomplished these actions today:

"Thought-habits can harden into character. So pay close attention to your thoughts." - The Buddha

In life, habits can have a deep impact on our character. The choices that we make in a day could lead to a habit that sticks with us forever. Thoughts are no different. Some thoughts today can become hardened into lifelong beliefs, and it's important to be mindful of this as things happen. Focusing as much as possible on the current moment, we may observe our thoughts carefully, and guard against those thoughts that reflect negatively on our character.

Today's Date:

This quote inspires the following thoughts in me:

This quote inspires me to take these actions today:

(Before bedtime) I accomplished these actions today:

"To him in whom love dwells, the whole world is but one family." - The Buddha

In a world that is often divisive and filled with violence, it can be difficult to always view others as connected to us - as family. That is not the case for Buddhists who believe in a philosophy of universal love. When we look at every person as a part of our global family, we are able to forgive those who have done wrong and move on from conflict with them.

Today's Date:

This quote inspires the following thoughts in me:

This quote inspires me to take these actions today:

(Before bedtime) I accomplished these actions today:

"To meditate is to listen with a receptive heart."
- The Buddha

Meditation isn't meant to be an escape from reality - just the opposite! It is a path to the ultimate reality. Meditation brings a person into a calm space where they can explore their thoughts and feelings more deeply than they otherwise would be able to. Do you meditate? How do you connect to that calm space within you every day?

Today's Date:

This quote inspires the following thoughts in me:

This quote inspires me to take these actions today:

(Before bedtime) I accomplished these actions today:

"Victory breeds hatred; the defeated live in pain. The peaceful live happily, giving up victory and defeat."
- The Buddha

We live in a world where winning and losing seems to be how people value each other, in sports, in business, in arguments, etc. How much better it would be if instead what we all valued was the peace and happiness that we could bring into the world. Will you reflect today on how winning and losing shapes the world you live in, and on how loving kindness can actually achieve more for the world?

Today's Date:

This quote inspires the following thoughts in me:

This quote inspires me to take these actions today:

(Before bedtime) I accomplished these actions today:

"Teach this triple truth to all: A generous heart, kind speech, and a life of service and compassion are the things which renew humanity." - The Buddha

The Buddha preached that generosity, kindness and service to others were vital in creating happiness and positive change in ourselves and for our society. Buddhism teaches that we should not only focus on ourselves but on the well-being of all people. The more we do good for others, the more we will be rewarded with happiness.

Today's Date:

This quote inspires the following thoughts in me:

This quote inspires me to take these actions today:

(Before bedtime) I accomplished these actions today:

"We begin to die from the moment we are born, for birth is the cause of death. The nature of decay is inherent in youth, the nature of sickness is inherent in health, in the midst of life we are truly in death."
- The Buddha

When we understand and accept that our life is in a constant state of change and decay, and that death may take us at any moment, we may find it easier to live fully and joyfully in this moment, without concern for the past or the future. All we have is now.

Today's Date:

This quote inspires the following thoughts in me:

This quote inspires me to take these actions today:

(Before bedtime) I accomplished these actions today:

"Intrinsically all living beings are Buddhas, endowed with wisdom and virtue, but because men's minds have become inverted through delusive thinking they fail to perceive this." - The Buddha

Enlightenment is available to each of us, because we are are humans, capable of reflection and insight. The Buddha was just a man who found the way through "delusive thinking," and he spent the next 50 years of his life trying to show how enlightenment is just waiting for discovery inside of us. Knowing that it is available to you, what steps will you take today to come closer to it?

Today's Date:

This quote inspires the following thoughts in me:

This quote inspires me to take these actions today:

(Before bedtime) I accomplished these actions today:

"I do not believe in a fate that falls on men however they act; but I do believe in a fate that falls on them unless they act." - The Buddha

Some people think that everything is predetermined by fate, while others are more inclined to think that our destiny is created by the choices we make throughout life. Are some people destined for greatness while others are destined to be failures? Should people assume that they are in control of their destiny if they make the right decisions, or should these individuals realize that they are still subject to fate?

Today's Date:

This quote inspires the following thoughts in me:

This quote inspires me to take these actions today:

(Before bedtime) I accomplished these actions today:

"Life is short. Spend it with people who make you laugh and feel loved." - The Buddha

We have a choice when it comes to who we spend time with. Why would we spend even one minute with people who don't bring us joy/ We would we spend one second with people who don't express kindness and compassion? It's easy to find people who would enjoy making you as unhappy as they are. Why would you give them the chance?

Today's Date:

This quote inspires the following thoughts in me:

This quote inspires me to take these actions today:

(Before bedtime) I accomplished these actions today:

"When it is impossible for anger to arise within you, you find no outside enemies anywhere." - The Buddha

The moment we start to face the full weight of our own human condition and the pain that arises from this, we no longer need anyone or anything else to blame for our suffering. We can love ourselves because we know that we don't deserve the pain that we've experienced and therefore other people don't deserve it either.

Today's Date:

This quote inspires the following thoughts in me:

This quote inspires me to take these actions today:

(Before bedtime) I accomplished these actions today:

"If you're helping someone and expecting something in return, you're doing business not kindness."
- The Buddha

We are used to living in a world of transactions. We go to the store and pay money for our food; we enter a contract with an employer to do work for a salary. But why should we share the compassion and kindness that is in our heart with someone, if we don't get back something in return from them? Answer this with your heart, and you'll be in the realm of the Buddha.

Today's Date:

This quote inspires the following thoughts in me:

This quote inspires me to take these actions today:

(Before bedtime) I accomplished these actions today:

"Happiness is not having a lot. Happiness is giving a lot." - The Buddha

How is it that many of the happiest people among us are those with the least? What do they know that the rest of us don't? The Buddha was born a prince, into a fabulous wealthy family, and was given every earthly desire. But he gave up literally everything he had to understand the truth of human existence. And when he became enlightened, he spent the next 50 years teaching his disciples, without ever asking for payment in return. What lesson is there in this for you?

Today's Date:

This quote inspires the following thoughts in me:

This quote inspires me to take these actions today:

(Before bedtime) I accomplished these actions today:

"Live every act fully, as if it were your last."
- The Buddha

Being centered and mindful encourages us to draw maximum joy from everything we do in this moment, even the simplest things. There is no guarantee of tomorrow, or even the next minute. Is it better to spend our life regretting the past, or concerned about the future, or is it better to spend each moment in the here and now, fully engaged in the joy of being alive right now?

Today's Date:

This quote inspires the following thoughts in me:

This quote inspires me to take these actions today:

(Before bedtime) I accomplished these actions today:

"All that we are is the result of what we have thought. The mind is everything. What we think we become."
- The Buddha

Do you believe it is possible for you to create the life that you want? Over the last few decades the authors of books like The Power of Intention and The Secret have said that it is. But their wisdom is not new - the Buddha and other sages for thousands of years have understood the power of your mind to create the universe you desire. Knowing this now, will you use your thoughts to create the world that you want?

Today's Date:

This quote inspires the following thoughts in me:

This quote inspires me to take these actions today:

(Before bedtime) I accomplished these actions today:

"Develop a mind that is vast like space, where experiences both pleasant and unpleasant can appear and disappear without conflict, struggle or harm. Rest in a mind like vast sky." - The Buddha

It can be difficult to let go of experiences that are unpleasant. This is why it is important for us to practice mindfulness meditation. When we live in the present moment, our minds do not get caught up on things that happened in the past or on future worries that might come our way; instead, we focus on what actually matters - this moment.

Today's Date:

This quote inspires the following thoughts in me:

This quote inspires me to take these actions today:

(Before bedtime) I accomplished these actions today:

"Live one day at a time. Keep your attention in present time. Have no expectations. Make no judgements and give up the need to know why things happen as they do. Give it up." - The Buddha

Observe the world as it is, and you will find true peace. Look inside of yourself first, be in this moment, and simply observe all that is going on inside you and outside of you in this moment. Acknowledge what has happened in the past, let go of your preconceived notions of how the world should be/what life should look like. You are where you are meant to be right now.

Today's Date:

This quote inspires the following thoughts in me:

This quote inspires me to take these actions today:

(Before bedtime) I accomplished these actions today:

"If you light a lamp for somebody, it will also brighten your path." - The Buddha

We are all here on Earth together, trying to find our way. Sometimes people can get stuck in the hardest moments of life, and feel hopeless. When you are faced with someone who is struggling, it's your responsibility to help them out of their despair. What goes around comes around. Your kindness and compassion will come back to you, and your own joy, peace, and happiness will grow.

Today's Date:

This quote inspires the following thoughts in me:

This quote inspires me to take these actions today:

(Before bedtime) I accomplished these actions today:

"My teaching is a means of practice, not something to hold onto or worship." - The Buddha

You may think you're struggling to find peace, happiness, and enlightenment. But you are really just looking in the wrong place. Buddha knows that you have all of these things inside of you if only you give yourself time to come to this realization. You may say you are not perfect or holy enough- but these are concepts that do not exist if you allow yourself to see the world through your Buddha's eyes.

Today's Date:

This quote inspires the following thoughts in me:

This quote inspires me to take these actions today:

(Before bedtime) I accomplished these actions today:

"A dog is not considered a good dog because he is a good barker. A man is not considered a good man because he is a good talker." - The Buddha

What is it then that makes you a good person? Is it your status in life? Is it the size of your bank account, or the kind of vehicle you drive? Or do you value more the good that you bring into the world through loving kindness and compassion? How do you value your own contribution to the world?

Today's Date:

This quote inspires the following thoughts in me:

This quote inspires me to take these actions today:

(Before bedtime) I accomplished these actions today:

"It is better to travel well than to arrive."
- The Buddha

Each of knows that our journey will end in death. So why don't we focus on the joys that can be found in this moment, before death comes for us? We all have a limited time on this earth. Why then do we spend so much time dwelling on the negative aspects of life? Why not focus on the moments of joy and laughter that we experience, since these are the times when we can feel most alive?

Today's Date:

This quote inspires the following thoughts in me:

This quote inspires me to take these actions today:

(Before bedtime) I accomplished these actions today:

"A fool who recognizes his own ignorance is thereby in fact a wise man, but a fool who considers himself wise – that is what one really calls a fool." - The Buddha

We all know people who believe they are they are the experts in the room. They spew forth endlessly with their self-serving drivel, never stopping to think how empty of wisdom they really are. Isn't it better to approach every moment with the mind of a beginner, always seeking the truth, always looking to fully experience everything afresh, and never assuming that we are right about everything?

Today's Date:

This quote inspires the following thoughts in me:

This quote inspires me to take these actions today:

(Before bedtime) I accomplished these actions today:

"A kind man who makes good use of wealth is rightly said to possess a great treasure; but the miser who hoards up his riches will have no profit" - The Buddha

How generous are you with your wealth, your knowledge, and your compassion? We all have something to share: our thoughts, feelings, knowledge, time, money - the list goes on. Sharing what we have connects us as human beings, and brings us joy in the moment, while bringing happiness and joy to the recipient as well. How will you share your wealth today?

Today's Date:

This quote inspires the following thoughts in me:

This quote inspires me to take these actions today:

(Before bedtime) I accomplished these actions today:

"Anyone who is not working toward the truth is missing the whole point of living." - The Buddha

Most people spend their time searching for meaning in outside sources and things (such as money, fame, and power) and fail to find it. Buddhists look deep within themselves and find purpose in life by following the simple teachings which teach virtues such as kindness, generosity, wisdom, and compassion.

Today's Date:

This quote inspires the following thoughts in me:

This quote inspires me to take these actions today:

(Before bedtime) I accomplished these actions today:

"As rain falls equally on the just and the unjust, do not burden your heart with judgments but rain your kindness equally on all." - The Buddha

This is a beautiful idea which can help us move past not only our own life's trials, but also the trials of others. It's easy to see why this quote resonates deeply with people - we are all imperfect humans who make mistakes, but there is always something we can do to make someone else's burden lighter.

Today's Date:

This quote inspires the following thoughts in me:

This quote inspires me to take these actions today:

(Before bedtime) I accomplished these actions today:

"Awake. Be the witness of your thoughts. The elephant hauls himself from the mud. In the same way drag yourself out of your sloth." - The Buddha

The only way to change a habitual mindset is to commit to being the witness of your thoughts. Dwelling on negative thoughts will not only have a detrimental impact on your mood, but it'll also lead you to feel drained and exhausted. In order to break free from this vicious cycle, you need to really get in touch with what's going on internally and take responsibility for your thoughts, rather than trying to push them away or deny their existence.

Today's Date:

This quote inspires the following thoughts in me:

This quote inspires me to take these actions today:

(Before bedtime) I accomplished these actions today:

"Before giving, the mind of the giver is happy; while giving, the mind of the giver is made peaceful; and having given, the mind of the giver is uplifted."
- The Buddha

By sharing our love, kindness, and compassion freely to others, we attract even more into our own life. Why then would we ever be unkind?

Today's Date:

This quote inspires the following thoughts in me:

This quote inspires me to take these actions today:

(Before bedtime) I accomplished these actions today:

"Believe, meditate, see. Be harmless, be blameless.
Awake to the law. And from all sorrows
free yourself." - The Buddha

Believe in your own potential, meditate on it and see the power within. You already have within you the ability to achieve the same enlightenment that the Buddha achieved. You already have within you the ability to live joyfully in every moment. Since the potential is already within you, why do you not seek it earnestly?

Today's Date:

This quote inspires the following thoughts in me:

This quote inspires me to take these actions today:

(Before bedtime) I accomplished these actions today:

"Change is never painful, only the resistance to change is painful." - The Buddha

It's easy to get comfortable in a routine. Doing the same thing over and over again, day after day, week after week, month after month. That is, until something forces us to change. People resist change because it can be difficult and stressful. However, if we can see change as an opportunity to grow and move forward with grace, it will not feel like pain at all.

Today's Date:

This quote inspires the following thoughts in me:

This quote inspires me to take these actions today:

(Before bedtime) I accomplished these actions today:

"Do not judge yourself harshly. Without mercy for ourselves we cannot love the world." - The Buddha

We are all humans, with both strengths and weaknesses. We all have the potential to grow, cultivate compassion, and cultivate wisdom. It's important to remember that when judging yourself. Without mercy for ourselves we cannot love the world. Taking time to reflect on our actions in an honest manner will help us find the root of our problems and allow us to grow in a way that benefits us and others around us.

Today's Date:

This quote inspires the following thoughts in me:

This quote inspires me to take these actions today:

(Before bedtime) I accomplished these actions today:

"Foolish, ignorant people indulge in careless lives, whereas a clever man guards his attention as his most precious possession." - The Buddha

Living in the present can be difficult when you are constantly thinking about the past or future. When you are fully present and mindful, it is much more joyful than being concerned with the past or future. This is because when you are living in the moment, you are experiencing all of life and not just snippets of it.

Today's Date:

This quote inspires the following thoughts in me:

This quote inspires me to take these actions today:

(Before bedtime) I accomplished these actions today:

"'He insulted me, he cheated me, he beat me, he robbed me' — those who are free of resentful thoughts surely find peace." - The Buddha

Resentment and anger are not emotions we enjoy having. However, we all experience them at some point in our lives. Whether it's because we didn't get what we deserved, someone wronged us, or something is unfair, resentment and anger can be strong and powerful emotions. If we allow these feelings to fester and grow, it can lead to an overwhelming sense of unhappiness and discontent.

Today's Date:

This quote inspires the following thoughts in me:

This quote inspires me to take these actions today:

(Before bedtime) I accomplished these actions today:

"How does one practice mindfulness? Sit in meditation. Be aware of only your breath."
- The Buddha

We are always on our phones or lost in thought; we rarely take the time to be present. The simplest way to slow down and enjoy life is through meditation. The way to be mindful is to sit in meditation and be aware of your breath. Keep returning your attention back to your breathing, and patiently maintain awareness on this single focus.

Today's Date:

This quote inspires the following thoughts in me:

This quote inspires me to take these actions today:

(Before bedtime) I accomplished these actions today:

"How wonderful! How wonderful! All things are perfect, exactly as they are." - The Buddha

The earth is perfect, it does what it needs to do, and never ceases to amaze us with its beauty and creativity. Our bodies are perfect too. We have everything we need for life right here inside of us, all the time. Do you believe this? If so, how can you worry about anything?

Today's Date:

This quote inspires the following thoughts in me:

This quote inspires me to take these actions today:

(Before bedtime) I accomplished these actions today:

"I teach one thing and one thing only: that is, suffering and the end of suffering." - The Buddha

The Buddha taught that suffering is a natural part of life and that living in the world with our five senses is like drinking salt water--we can't avoid the salty taste. However, he also told us that we have the power to shape our lives so they are not all suffering. His goal for people's lives was a mindful one with a clear intention of compassion and kindness. For such a simple concept, why is it so difficult for us to attain?

Today's Date:

This quote inspires the following thoughts in me:

This quote inspires me to take these actions today:

(Before bedtime) I accomplished these actions today:

"If a man speaks or acts with a pure thought, happiness follows him, like a shadow that never leaves him." - The Buddha

When we focus on our thoughts and actions to be as positive as possible, we can see how this quote proves true. There is an endless well of joy and peace to be found in our minds and actions if we put forth the effort to find it. We have control over our own happiness and unhappiness. Why would we choose unhappiness?

Today's Date:

This quote inspires the following thoughts in me:

This quote inspires me to take these actions today:

(Before bedtime) I accomplished these actions today:

"If we can look upon our work not for self-benefit, but as a means to benefit society, we will be practicing appreciation and patience in our daily lives."
- The Buddha

If we engage in work that does not benefit society in some positive way, we are only serving ourselves. The Buddha taught that "Right Livelihood" - the fourth step on the Eight Fold Path - is to choose a job that does not produce suffering for oneself or others. Examine what it is you do for a living. Are you comfortable that it satisfies the definition of Right Livelihood?

Today's Date:

This quote inspires the following thoughts in me:

This quote inspires me to take these actions today:

(Before bedtime) I accomplished these actions today:

"Imagine that every person in the world is enlightened but you. They are all your teachers, each doing just the right things to help you." - The Buddha

The concept of "beginner's mind" is an important Buddhist philosophy. It is the idea that one should find joy in the process of learning. It's not about what you know but how much you are willing to learn. The term describes the innocence and openness of a new learner to see everything with fresh eyes. Is this how you see the world?

Today's Date:

This quote inspires the following thoughts in me:

This quote inspires me to take these actions today:

(Before bedtime) I accomplished these actions today:

"Joyously participate in the sorrows of others."
- The Buddha

On first reading, this quote sounds a bit ghoulish! It seems to be an oxymoron. But the truth is that the Buddha is challenging us to live a life of compassion and understanding, whatever the circumstances. We can share our joy by offering sympathy and understanding to someone who is grieving. Our joy should be spread so no one goes without love or kindness or compassion.

Today's Date:

This quote inspires the following thoughts in me:

This quote inspires me to take these actions today:

(Before bedtime) I accomplished these actions today:

"Just as a solid rock is not shaken by the storm, even so the wise are not affected by praise or blame."
- The Buddha

It is easy, and can be tempting, to allow your ego to be inflated by praise. And yet, those who take the time to remain humble often find that their careers thrive. They remain grounded and work hard to improve themselves, as opposed to those who rely on their inflated ego as a crutch. Is it possible to treat praise or blame without our egos becoming inflated or hurt?

Today's Date:

This quote inspires the following thoughts in me:

This quote inspires me to take these actions today:

(Before bedtime) I accomplished these actions today:

"Let us live in joy, never falling sick like those who hate us. Let us live in freedom, without hatred even among those who hate." - The Buddha

It's too easy for us to fall into the same frame of mind or bad mood as the people around us, but it's important to resist this temptation and stay grounded in this moment. We can't let what has already happened cloud what is happening now. We must stay in the joy of this moment, and work to be an example to those who are not yet there.

Today's Date:

This quote inspires the following thoughts in me:

This quote inspires me to take these actions today:

(Before bedtime) I accomplished these actions today:

"Look within, thou art the the Buddha."
- The Buddha

This quote is an example of Buddhist philosophy encouraging people to see their own wisdom and personal happiness by looking inward. The Buddha taught that he was just a human, not a god, and that what he had achieved is available to every human on the earth if they strive for enlightenment. Knowing that you are the Buddha too, how will your day be different today?

Today's Date:

This quote inspires the following thoughts in me:

This quote inspires me to take these actions today:

(Before bedtime) I accomplished these actions today:

"May I meet the suffering and ignorance of others with compassion." - The Buddha

The most important thing that you can do when you encounter someone who is suffering is to offer them your compassion. A compassionate heart is the source of happiness for oneself and for others. When you focus on being compassionate, rather than being selfish, your life will be full of more meaning. And if you are not trapped in your own suffering, then you can see that there are many people who are suffering just like you.

Today's Date:

This quote inspires the following thoughts in me:

This quote inspires me to take these actions today:

(Before bedtime) I accomplished these actions today:

"Neither my life of luxury in the palace -nor- my life as ascetic in the forest were ways to enlightenment."
- The Buddha

Before he became the Buddha, Siddhartha Gautama was a prince, surrounded by luxury, and without knowledge of the suffering in the world. After he left his palace to uncover the meaning behind human suffering, he spent seven years living as an ascetic - someone who renounces all material possessions and physical pleasures. But it wasn't until he found the "Middle Path" that Gautama achieved enlightenment. He discovered that expressing the love and compassion each of us has within us is the only way to happiness. Now we know the answer. We will follow his path?

Today's Date:

This quote inspires the following thoughts in me:

This quote inspires me to take these actions today:

(Before bedtime) I accomplished these actions today:

"A mind unruffled by the vagaries of fortune, from sorrow freed, from defilements cleansed, from fear liberated — this is the greatest blessing." - The Buddha

For all who are interested in realizing their deepest potential, the greatest blessing is to be free from mental duress. There are many paths to achieving this state of mind, however they all hinge on one thing: detachment. One way to detach is by taking refuge in the Buddhist path. Buddha asserts that it is through the cultivation of mindfulness and awareness that one can transcend pain, sorrow, fear, and defilements.

Today's Date:

This quote inspires the following thoughts in me:

This quote inspires me to take these actions today:

(Before bedtime) I accomplished these actions today:

"When you attain victory over yourself, not even the gods can turn it into defeat." - The Buddha

One of the core principles in Buddhism is that its followers must work to improve themselves rather than look outside for help or guidance. Buddha wanted his followers to conquer their human nature and become enlightened by turning inward instead of relying on outside forces for happiness or fulfillment.

Today's Date:

This quote inspires the following thoughts in me:

This quote inspires me to take these actions today:

(Before bedtime) I accomplished these actions today:

"You should respect each other and refrain from disputes; you should not, like water and oil, repel each other, but should, like milk and water, mingle together." - The Buddha

Dealing with difficult people can be a challenge. You often find that you must interact with these people despite the fact that they just seem to rub us the wrong way and we don't understand why. It is important to handle these encounters in a way that leaves us feeling empowered and not drained. Can you be the better person in the relationship? Can you engage with someone who gets on your nerves with compassion and kindness?

Today's Date:

This quote inspires the following thoughts in me:

This quote inspires me to take these actions today:

(Before bedtime) I accomplished these actions today:

"Kindness should become the natural way of life,
not the exception." - The Buddha

Share your kindness and compassion every day, everywhere. It's thoughtful gestures that are often times unseen but are cherished nonetheless. A smile, a gesture, a helping hand, these small things make the world a better place. When thoughtfulness becomes natural, it will become as easy as drinking a cool glass of water on a hot day. Use your kindness to quench a world thirsty for it.

Today's Date:

This quote inspires the following thoughts in me:

This quote inspires me to take these actions today:

(Before bedtime) I accomplished these actions today:

"As you travel through life, offer good wishes to each being you meet." - The Buddha

Whether it's a stranger on the street or a loved one, we can show them kindness and compassion and wish them peace and happiness. These simple gestures of goodwill can go a long way in improving our own peace of mind and happiness. A little bit of love is all it takes to make this world a better place for everyone.

Today's Date:

This quote inspires the following thoughts in me:

This quote inspires me to take these actions today:

(Before bedtime) I accomplished these actions today:

"Rage is a powerful energy that with diligent practice can be transformed into fierce compassion. However much we disagree with our enemies, our task is to identify with them." - The Buddha

Anger and frustration are the natural response to the belief that we have been harmed by those who do not share our values or interests. The practice of patience and compassion is not easy, but with diligent application it can be achieved. Our task should be to identify with the suffering of our enemies rather than disagreeing with them, and thereby transform harmful energy into kindness and compassion.

Today's Date:

This quote inspires the following thoughts in me:

This quote inspires me to take these actions today:

(Before bedtime) I accomplished these actions today:

"Happiness will never come to those who fail to appreciate what they already have." - The Buddha

You are what you think. If you think positive thoughts, you will be happy. Happiness is not something that can be found by chasing after it, but rather it is something that you must subconsciously make the effort to maintain. The pursuit of happiness is a lifelong journey. You must appreciate what you have now in order to create the life that you want for yourself in the future.

Today's Date:

This quote inspires the following thoughts in me:

This quote inspires me to take these actions today:

(Before bedtime) I accomplished these actions today:

"Happy people build their inner world. Unhappy people blame their outer world." - The Buddha

People who are happy with their lives and the people in it tend to be happy no matter what is happening outside of them. Conversely, unhappy people tend to look to their external world for happiness and blame that for their unhappiness. This leads to an unhealthy cycle where they produce negative thoughts that create more negativity which leads back to blaming the outer world. If you are unhappy, stop blaming the outer world and accept responsibility for your own happiness.

Today's Date:

This quote inspires the following thoughts in me:

This quote inspires me to take these actions today:

(Before bedtime) I accomplished these actions today:

"Happiness is not having a lot. Happiness is giving a lot." - The Buddha

Many of us often find ourselves in a state of euphoria when we acquire something new and shiny to add to our lives. However, this happiness is fleeting. True, long-lasting happiness comes from spreading love and compassion to the people in our lives and in the world around us.

Today's Date:

This quote inspires the following thoughts in me:

This quote inspires me to take these actions today:

(Before bedtime) I accomplished these actions today:

"Happiness is when what you think, what you say and what you do are in harmony." - The Buddha

In order to be happy, it is important to live in harmony with one's thoughts, words and actions. Too often, people will do something they know is bad for them or say things they know are not true simply because they think it will make them happy. In reality, the only way to truly attain happiness is by living in accordance with what you know is right and good.

Today's Date:

This quote inspires the following thoughts in me:

This quote inspires me to take these actions today:

(Before bedtime) I accomplished these actions today:

"I am the owner of my actions, heir to my actions, related through my actions, and have my actions as my arbitrator. Whatever I do, for good or for evil, to that I will fall heir." - The Buddha

Are you really in control? We decide what we do and how we do it, and we live with the consequences. What we do is an extension of who we are and our values and principles. This is what makes us human - our actions and their consequences.

Today's Date:

This quote inspires the following thoughts in me:

This quote inspires me to take these actions today:

(Before bedtime) I accomplished these actions today:

"When we feel happy and peaceful, our happiness and peace radiates around us, and others can enjoy it as well." - The Buddha

People who are more mindful experience greater happiness and peace, which is in turn sent out to those around them. People who are mindful breath deeply, notice their surroundings, focus on what they are doing in the moment, and don't worry about things they cannot control. By practicing mindfulness techniques, we can positively influence everything that happens around us.

Today's Date:

<u>This quote inspires the following thoughts in me:</u>

<u>This quote inspires me to take these actions today:</u>

<u>(Before bedtime) I accomplished these actions today:</u>

357

"When you dig a well, there's no sign of water until you reach it, only rocks and dirt to move out of the way. When you have removed enough, soon the pure water will flow." - The Buddha

The most important things in life often come to us only through long hours of concentrated and difficult work. But when the work is accomplished, we are rewarded. Are you willing to put in the hard work to achieve joy and happiness in your life?

Today's Date:

This quote inspires the following thoughts in me:

This quote inspires me to take these actions today:

(Before bedtime) I accomplished these actions today:

"Why cling to the pain and the wrongs of yesterday?
Why hold on to the very things that keep you from
hope and love?" - The Buddha

Clinging to the pain of yesterday is what keeps us from experiencing hopefulness and joy. For many people, it becomes a vicious cycle of thinking about what has happened in the past, but not being able to move forward because of this. It can be difficult at first, but with self-compassion, eventually one will learn to let go of these feelings and be able to move into a much more contented life.

Today's Date:

This quote inspires the following thoughts in me:

This quote inspires me to take these actions today:

(Before bedtime) I accomplished these actions today:

"The less you have, the less you have to worry about."
- The Buddha

The suffering we encounter in our lives can be reduced if we detach ourselves from material things and focus on cultivating mindfulness and awareness. This approach is often referred to as "living mindfully." The Buddha taught that material wealth and indulging in worldly pleasures is not a path toward enlightenment, but rather attachment to those things will increase one's suffering.

Today's Date:

This quote inspires the following thoughts in me:

This quote inspires me to take these actions today:

(Before bedtime) I accomplished these actions today:

"When you find no solution to a problem, it's probably not a problem to be solved, but rather a truth to be accepted." - The Buddha

Everyone reaches a point in their life where they feel like they are facing an insurmountable problem. It can be an emotional issue, crisis of faith, or a big project. There is always something challenging life throws at us, and when we face it head on, we can often find the lesson in our problem. Look for the lessons in every problem you face. You just might find wisdom there.

Today's Date:

This quote inspires the following thoughts in me:

This quote inspires me to take these actions today:

(Before bedtime) I accomplished these actions today:

"Patience is key. Remember: A jug fills drop by drop."
- The Buddha

Did you ever feel like something was too hard, or not worth the time or effort required to accomplish it? If you knew that there was something vitally important to learn by see the work through, would you find the fortitude inside you to continue? Wisdom doesn't come all at once. Keep going.

Today's Date:

This quote inspires the following thoughts in me:

This quote inspires me to take these actions today:

(Before bedtime) I accomplished these actions today:

"The true master lives in truth, in goodness and restraint, non-violence, moderation, and purity."
- The Buddha

She who cultivates her mind so that it's not mired in greed, hatred or delusion is a moral person who knows the world is created on the principle of cause and effect. In this way she doesn't have to worry about evil. Goodness is an innate quality of human beings but something we must choose to practice.

Today's Date:

This quote inspires the following thoughts in me:

This quote inspires me to take these actions today:

(Before bedtime) I accomplished these actions today:

"In our lives, change is unavoidable, loss is unavoidable. In the adaptability and ease with which we experience change, lies our happiness and freedom." - The Buddha

When we live in the moment, the constancy of change becomes in some respects comforting. Good and bad things happen, we are happy and then sad, we have good fortune for a while and then lose it all. It's in our ability to let go of things in our past and embrace new things in the future that we find peace in the chaos of life.

Today's Date:

This quote inspires the following thoughts in me:

This quote inspires me to take these actions today:

(Before bedtime) I accomplished these actions today:

"There is only one time when it is essential to awaken. That time is now." - The Buddha

What are you waiting for? We all have both the ability and the responsibility to explore our inner life in order to find our own truth. The best way to fully explore your inner life is through meditation, which will guide you on how best to live your life and become the best version of yourself. You have this moment. Do not waste it, because there is no guarantee of a next moment. What are you waiting for?

Today's Date:

This quote inspires the following thoughts in me:

This quote inspires me to take these actions today:

(Before bedtime) I accomplished these actions today:

Made in United States
Troutdale, OR
04/24/2024

19428608R00210